A
Confident
Heart
Devotional

Also by Renee Swope

A Confident Heart
A Confident Heart DVD
Encouragement for Today

A
Confident
Heart
Devotional

60 Days to Stop Doubting Yourself

Renee Swope

Revell

a division of Baker Publishing Group
Grand Rapids, Michigan

Published by Revell
a division of Baker Publishing Group
P.O. Box 6287, Grand Rapids, MI 49516-6287
www.revellbooks.com

Printed in the United States of America

Library of Congress Cataloging-in-Publication Data is on file at the Library of Congress, Washington, DC.

ISBN 978-0-8007-2243-2 (pbk.)

Unless otherwise indicated, Scripture quotations are from the Holy Bible, New International Version®. NIV®. Copyright © 1973, 1978, 1984, 2011 by Biblica, Inc.™ Used by permission of Zondervan. All rights reserved worldwide. www.zondervan.com

Scripture quotations labeled AMP are from the Amplified® Bible, copyright © 1954, 1958, 1962, 1964, 1965, 1987 by The Lockman Foundation. Used by permission.

Scripture quotations labeled CEV are from the Contemporary English Version © 1991, 1992, 1995 by American Bible Society. Used by permission.

Scripture quotations labeled GW are from GOD'S WORD®. © 1995 God's Word to the Nations. Used by permission of Baker Publishing Group.

Scripture quotations labeled Message are from *The Message* by Eugene H. Peterson, copyright © 1993, 1994, 1995, 2000, 2001, 2002. Used by permission of NavPress Publishing Group. All rights reserved.

Scripture quotations labeled NASB are from the New American Standard Bible®, copyright © 1960, 1962, 1963, 1968, 1971, 1972, 1973, 1975, 1977, 1995 by The Lockman Foundation. Used by permission.

Scripture quotations labeled NLT are from the *Holy Bible*, New Living Translation, copyright © 1996, 2004, 2007 by Tyndale House Foundation. Used by permission of Tyndale House Publishers, Inc., Carol Stream, Illinois 60188. All rights reserved.

Published in association with The Fedd Agency, 317 Ranch Road 620 South, Suite 100A, Austin, TX 78734

In keeping with biblical principles of creation stewardship, Baker Publishing Group advocates the responsible use of our natural resources. As a member of the Green Press Initiative, our company uses recycled paper when possible. The text paper of this book is composed in part of post-consumer waste.

13   14   15   16   17   18   19   7   6   5   4   3   2   1

Contents

CONTENTS

From My Heart to Yours

As I imagine you reading this page, I wish we were sitting in a coffee shop chatting. I would love to talk with you about things that may be weighing you down. They always seem to lighten when shared with a friend. I would tell you about the times I let my doubts pile up, and how the weight of my worries almost took me down.

And you just might hear the story about the time I accidentally took my dog's medication. Yes. I sure did. Hopefully, knowing that little fact about me would make you feel a little better about yourself.

There is nothing more reassuring for a woman than realizing she is not the only one who struggles with doubt, fear, or any array of emotions and imperfections she's convinced herself that other women don't have.

And in that moment we sometimes wonder if maybe—just maybe—that friend who let us know she struggles too could walk beside us as we try to find our way out of the shadow of our doubts.

I have had that kind of friend, and I would love to be *that* kind of friend for you.

But since we can't chat in a coffee shop, I'm hoping we can meet right here on the pages of this book for the next sixty days. I'd love to tell you just how normal and wonderful you are, and help you take hold of truths that will unfold the plans and promises God has for your life.

Over the past several years, God has been changing me and rearranging me, using His Word and His unconditional love to lead me to what I call God-fidence. It's a deep-down soul-security that has little to do with what we do or don't have but everything to do with all God is and all that He offers us each day.

Through stories of men and women in the Bible who battled insecurity and fear, I've discovered it's possible to stop doubting myself and to start living, by faith, in the security of God's promises, no matter what my circumstances or emotions tell me.

Using powerful promises from His Word, I've created a new thought-map. And I use it every day to redirect my thinking, to make sure my heart is being led by truth. At the end of each devotion I'll share one of these promises that ties in to the topic of the day, so you can use His thoughts to redirect yours all day.

I've also asked a few friends to share their stories throughout the book, so you can be inspired by their journey and learn from their process of finding confidence in Christ.

Each morning, I hope you'll grab your Bible and meet with me here. I can't wait to encourage you and walk beside you as you step out from the shadows of your doubt and learn to live with a confident heart!

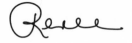

1

Turning Points

You are a chosen [woman], a royal [priest], a holy [daughter], God's special possession, that you may declare the praises of him who called you out of the darkness into his wonderful light.

1 Peter 2:9

I stood in front of my bathroom mirror, getting ready to travel to a large event while begging God to zap me with confidence—or send Jesus back before it was time for me to speak. I had been struggling with paralyzing self-doubt that week and it was making me question everything.

When I turned to put something in my suitcase, which was behind me, I noticed a huge nine-foot shadow on the wall. I was surprised how big the shadow was and how much it distorted the image of my five-foot-two-inch frame.

In that moment, I realized my uncertainty had also created a huge shadow—a shadow of doubt that was distorting my thoughts and overpowering my emotions.

As I stood there looking at that humongous shadow, I sensed God telling me I could only see the shadow because I had turned away from the light.

Slowly I turned back toward the light above the mirror, and I was no longer standing in the shadow. But the fact that I had *created* the shadow by blocking the light taught me a powerful lesson—a truth that became a turning point for me.

Shadows are created all around us whenever something blocks the light. And so it is with the shadow of doubt. When we focus on how inadequate we feel, or what others are thinking about us, we cast a shadow of doubt in our minds by blocking the light of God's truth in our hearts.

Yet we were not designed to block the light or to be the light. We were created to live in the light, by finding our confidence in what God thinks about us.

Before that day in my bathroom with God and my shadow, I saw doubt as an annoying weakness, a lapse of faith, a dip in my self-confidence. And I just wanted God to take it away. But through my doubt, God led me to dependence on Him and taught me a powerful lesson that became a turning point in my life.

A shadow of self-doubt had been cast over my thoughts and emotions when I turned my attention away from God's perspective and promises. By taking my eyes off the light of God's truth, I ended up paralyzed by the darkness of defeat.

How about you? How often do you agree with the whispers of doubt and find yourself living in discouragement and uncertainty?

That day in my bathroom was a turning point where God equipped me with a powerful way to process and conquer self-doubts. And, as we take this sixty-day journey together, I want each day to be a turning point for you . . .

- As you turn toward God, so you can know who He is and His heart toward you.

- As you turn toward His truth, so you can listen to what God says about you and what He can do through you as you learn to depend more on Him.
- As you turn toward the light of God's promises as a woman, a friend, a leader, and a follower of Jesus—so your life can be about living, loving, and leading others to the light of God's truth as you walk it out in your everyday life.

When we turn our focus away from feelings of inadequacy and uncertainty and intentionally turn our thoughts toward God's promises of all-sufficiency, we create a turning point and we begin to replace our wavering self-confidence with lasting God-confidence. In doing so, our lives become a response to the One who has called us out of darkness into His wonderful light (1 Pet. 2:9).

So, are you ready to start turning?

Lord, I want to take Your hand and trust Your heart as You lead me on this sixty-day journey of overcoming self-doubt and living in the power of Your promises! You say I am a chosen woman and a holy daughter who belongs to You. If doubt overshadows my thoughts today, help me turn back to the light of Your truth, so I can focus on all I have in You. In Jesus' name, Amen.

When I say: My doubts won't go away.

God **says:** I am calling you out of the darkness. Turn toward the light and truth of what I say about you.

You are a chosen [woman], a royal [priest], a holy [daughter], God's special possession, that you may declare the praises of him who called you out of the darkness into his wonderful light. (1 Pet. 2:9)

2

How Did I Get Here?

But blessed is the one who trusts in the LORD, whose confidence is in him.

Jeremiah 17:7

---

*I*f only becoming a Christian meant all of our doubts and fears went away. Have you ever wondered why you struggle with insecurities and self-doubts though you know you are a child of God?

Maybe God is leading you to do something but doubt has convinced you you're not smart enough or gifted enough. Perhaps you wanted kids and now you have a family, but now you question if you have what it takes to be a good mom. Or maybe you've wanted to change jobs and now have the opportunity, but doubt you will succeed at something new.

In yesterday's devotion, I described the day I discovered the shadow of my doubt. After begging God to zap me with confidence and seeing that He wasn't going to do it, I asked Him to show me what made me start feeling so insecure. I wanted to know how I got to that yucky place of uncertainty.

Immediately I thought about Gideon, a man who was called by God yet was paralyzed by fear and inadequacy.

From reading his story in Judges 6, I knew Gideon overcame his doubts and fears by focusing on what God thought about him instead of what he thought about himself. But first, Gideon processed his doubts with God in a very honest way. He told the angel of the Lord that he questioned God's presence and doubted His promises because of recent conflicts and defeats.

It was time for me to get honest with God too. I needed more than a quick fix; I needed to figure out how I got into such a yucky place of uncertainty.

Earlier that week a conflict with a friend had made me doubt whether I should even be in ministry. *After all*, self-doubt whispered, *if I can't maintain healthy relationships at all times in all areas, how can I help others?* I had also received feedback on a project that week. Although there were several positive comments, one harsh criticism overshadowed the compliments and consumed my focus.

I had also fallen into the comparison trap and caught myself comparing my abilities as a speaker to others who'd been booked for an upcoming event with me. Self-doubt convinced me I wasn't as gifted as they were.

Conflict, criticism, and comparison had sent me into the shadows of doubt.

What about you? When conflict arises at home or at work, do you ever assume it disqualifies you from other ministries or callings? Does criticism ever paralyze you from believing you can do certain things? Has comparison ever convinced you that someone else can do it (whatever "it" is) better than you can?

Overcoming self-doubt is not a quick fix but a powerful process that begins when we start to identify our doubts, ask God and ourselves what triggered them, and then replace them with God's promises.

The next time you start feeling uncertain or insecure, stop and ask God to help you identify what thoughts triggered the doubt. Then ask Him to help you process your thoughts through the filter of His perspective.

Ask Him if there are lies you believe that need to be replaced with His truth. Then change your thought process by focusing on His thoughts toward you. For instance:

- When doubt tells you that you can't do something because it's too hard, remember God says you can do all things through Christ who strengthens you (Phil. 4:13).
- When doubt tells you that you're not good enough, focus on the truth that God says you're fearfully and wonderfully made; all of His works are wonderful and you are one of them (Ps. 139:14).

Over the next few days, we're going to look at Gideon's story and learn from the process God took him through to help him (and me) overcome paralyzing doubts and fears.

One thing you can be sure of: God wants to give you confidence for whatever you face! Some days it will be about what He's calling you to do, but oftentimes it will be about what He wants to do in you—as you learn to completely depend on Him.

Lord, I'm tired of feeling paralyzed by insecurity and uncertainty. Help me identify what triggers self-doubt and replace my thoughts with Your thoughts about me. I want to rely on and live in the security of Your promises. In Jesus' name, Amen.

When I say: Why do I still struggle with self-doubt?

God **says:** It takes time to overcome lifelong doubt. Let's walk through the process of finding your confidence through your relationship with Me.

> But blessed is the one who trusts in the Lord,
> whose confidence is in him. (Jer. 17:7)

3

When Life Is Hard

"Pardon me, my lord," Gideon replied, "but if the Lord
is with us, why has all this happened to us?"

Judges 6:13

---

o you ever ask God why life has to be so hard? Why certain things happen?

I asked God lots of questions during what I call my "year of impossible." A month after we brought our daughter home from Ethiopia, my mom was hospitalized with pulmonary embolisms, my dad had to have emergency quadruple bypass heart surgery, I had an abnormal mammogram that led to multiple biopsies, and a close friend died of breast cancer—all within six months.

I remember thinking, *Why has all this happened? Why does life have to be so hard?*

It's easy for me to feel abandoned during those times. I wonder where God is and why He isn't helping me. I think this might be how Gideon felt after all he had been through with the Midianites.

When the angel of the Lord appeared to Gideon, he said, "The Lord is with you, mighty warrior" (Judg. 6:12).

And Gideon responded with lots of questions: "Pardon me, my lord . . . but if the LORD is with us, why has all this happened to us? Where are all his wonders that our ancestors told us about when they said, 'Did not the LORD bring us up out of Egypt?' But now the LORD has abandoned us and given us into the hand of Midian" (v. 13).

So how did God answer Gideon's questions? "The LORD turned to him and said, 'Go in the strength you have and save Israel out of Midian's hand. Am I not sending you?'" (v. 14).

Notice how God didn't answer Gideon's "why" question. Instead God told him what role He was calling Gideon to play in what He was about to do next.

Perhaps God had already explained through the prophet that Gideon's trials and hard circumstances were the consequences of his family's sin. Sometimes when we ask God why, He shows us how our sin played a role in whatever is happening. Other times it's much harder to process, because the trouble isn't caused by anything we or anyone else has done. My friend and author Lysa TerKeurst says, "Asking why is perfectly normal. Asking why isn't unspiritual. However, if asking this question pushes us farther from God rather than drawing us closer to Him, it's the wrong question."[1]

I'm learning to embrace my unanswered "why" questions, and I'm realizing that sometimes life is hard because we live in a fallen world or we're experiencing a spiritual attack. Other times life is hard because we're not listening to God or following what He has shown us, as was the case for both the Israelites and me.

When life is hard, though, we are more likely to ask for God's help. I know it's true for me and for others I've talked to. Tough times often precipitate movement toward God and help us depend on Him more than on ourselves.

God used Gideon's "why" question to draw Gideon closer to Himself by shifting Gideon's focus from the hard things that had happened in his past to what God was about to do in his future.

God told Gideon he was going to be part of making things better by saving Israel from the Midianites.

Sometimes God answers our prayers by calling us to be part of the solution to our problems. Instead of changing our circumstances, often God uses our circumstances to change us by bringing us closer to Him, making us more like Him, and helping us find our confidence in Him.

Jesus, I get frustrated when life is hard and troubles abound. But I don't want that frustration to push me away from You. If my circumstances can't change, use them to change me—by bringing me closer to You, making me more like You, and helping me find my confidence in You through the circumstances I'm in. In Jesus' name, Amen.

When I say: My life is too hard.

God **says:** I am with you in the middle of these trials. I will not leave you nor forsake you.

I will be with [you] in trouble, I will deliver [you] and honor [you]. (Ps. 91:15)

4

Getting Past Our Past

*Forget the former things; do not dwell on the past. See, I
am doing a new thing! Now it springs up; do you not per-
ceive it? I am making a way in the wilderness and streams
in the wasteland.*

Isaiah 43:18–19

---

*A*re there negative things from your childhood or family history that have cast a shadow of doubt over your
destiny?

As a young girl, I felt like my family was broken and I was too.
When I was growing up, I knew very few people whose parents
were divorced. Since mine were, I felt "less than" when I was with
friends whose families were whole and happy.

Not only did I feel "less than," we had less than most people I
knew. Although my dad had a big, fancy house, my brothers and
I lived with my mom in a very modest duplex and drove a station
wagon that had more dents in it than the moon. We called it "the
wreck." I don't know how the dirt got in there, or why it stayed in

there, but I remember we had little weeds growing in the back of our station wagon. Seriously.

It's funny now, but it was embarrassing as a kid! Making things worse, my dad wouldn't pay child support, which made me think we must not be worth enough for him to take care of us.

When doubt washes over me, often it is because something has happened to activate my old emotions and create thoughts in my mind that are similar to those I had as a child. Sometimes that hurt little girl still has too much say in my heart. If I listen to her for too long, powerful yet immature emotions start rising to the surface from my past. But they are not truth in my life.

The insecurities from your past are not the truth in your life either. As you look at your doubts and develop a confident heart, it's important to recognize and examine negative emotions from your past that could keep you from living confidently in your present and future.

Our friend Gideon struggled with his self-image based on his family's history and his perception of himself. We see this in his response when the angel of the Lord told him God was going to use him to save his people. Gideon questioned him:

> "Pardon me, my lord," Gideon replied, "but how can I save Israel? My clan is the weakest in Manasseh, and I am the least in my family." (Judg. 6:15)

His past made him question God's promises for his future. Damaged emotions and insecurities from our past have a powerful influence over how we see ourselves today.

Once we become daughters of the King, we have a royal inheritance that determines who we are. Our family of origin reflects our lineage but it does not define our heritage. Whether we had a great family or not, our hearts will only find lasting confidence when we find our complete identity in our inheritance as children of God.

Gideon had to stop thinking of himself as the runt of his family and start seeing himself as a child of God, a mighty warrior in his Father's eyes. Although he was tempted to look back, God challenged him to look ahead. He could see beyond who Gideon was to who he could become.

God promised Gideon he would defeat his enemies, and he would not fight alone. "The LORD answered, 'I will be with you, and you will strike down all the Midianites, leaving none alive'" (v. 16).

Gideon's first steps out of the shadow of doubt would require he get past his past by addressing his insecurities about it—but not dwelling on it. Gideon chose to trust God's heart by depending on God's strength instead of his own. He shifted his focus from doubting himself to believing his God.

More than just helping him conquer the Midianites, God helped Gideon overcome his past and conquer his personal enemies of doubt and fear. And He wants to do the same things in our lives.

Oftentimes God will use our doubts to build our confidence by calling us to face our fears and do something we would never choose on our own. But when we depend on Him, we experience victory we never thought possible!

Lord, I need courage and strength to overcome insecurities from my past so they don't hold me back anymore. Help me trust You with my heart. In Jesus' name, Amen.

When I say: I can't get past my past.

God **says:** Let Me help you heal from your past so it doesn't hinder the plans I have for your future. I want to do a new thing in you.

> Forget the former things; do not dwell on the past. See, I am doing a new thing! Now it springs up; do you not perceive it? I am making a way in the wilderness and streams in the wasteland. (Isa. 43:18–19)

5

My Image of God

Those who know your name trust you, O Lord, because
you have never deserted those who seek your help.

Psalm 9:10 GW

I didn't grow up knowing about God's love. In fact, my childhood perception of God was that He was distant and unapproachable. In my mind, He was standing on the sidelines of life keeping score of the ways I failed or disappointed Him.

Sadly, I think I created God in my father's image. You see, my dad showed disappointment through withdrawal and anger. When life was hard and I was lonely, I wondered what I'd done wrong and if God was mad at me.

My father showed love by buying me things. When good things happened in my life, I felt God's approval.

While reading Gideon's story and looking for patterns that matched my own struggle with doubt and fear, I noticed he didn't really know the heart of God either. Gideon's image of God included feelings of abandonment and disappointment.

When the angel of the Lord appeared to him in the winepress, Gideon asked: "Where are all [God's] wonders that our ancestors told us about when they said, 'Did not the LORD bring us up out of Egypt?' But now the LORD has abandoned us and given us into the hand of Midian" (Judg. 6:13).

Although God assured Gideon He would go with him and give him strength to defeat the Midianites, Gideon didn't trust God. It's hard to trust someone you don't really know.

> Gideon replied, "If now I have found favor in your eyes, give me a sign that it is really you talking to me. Please do not go away until I come back and bring my offering and set it before you."
> And the LORD said, "I will wait until you return." (vv. 17–18)

When Gideon brought his offering, the angel of the Lord touched it with the tip of his staff and fire flared from the rock, consuming it. Gideon exclaimed, "Alas, Sovereign LORD! I have seen the angel of the LORD face to face!" (v. 22).

Up to this point, Gideon had called Him "Lord." Now he used the word "Sovereign" to describe his Lord after experiencing God's sovereignty. Another layer of confidence was built when Gideon witnessed God's power.

However, Gideon must have looked terrified, because immediately "the LORD said to him, 'Peace! Do not be afraid'" (v. 23).

I love what happened next: "Gideon built an altar to the LORD there and called it The LORD Is Peace" (v. 24).

Notice how Gideon's image of God was transformed as he came to know God's character and His heart by experiencing His power and peace in personal ways.

The same is true for you and me. We may know many things about God, but we won't really know God's heart until we spend time with Him, talking, listening, and experiencing who He is. Our depth of trusting God comes when we depend on Him and discover that He is dependable, like Gideon did.

One of the ways we can learn to trust God is by getting to know Him the way He is described in the Bible, based on His names that reflect a promise of who He is.

We will know God as *Jehovah Rapha*, our Healer, as we experience and recognize His healing in our lives—spiritually, emotionally, mentally, and physically.

We will know Him as *Jehovah Jireh*, our Provider, when we depend on Him to meet our needs. We will know Him as *El Shaddai*, the All-Sufficient God, when we allow His sufficiency to fill in the gaps of our inadequacy.

Let's grow in our confidence as we live in the promise: "Those who know your name trust you, O Lord, because you have never deserted those who seek your help" (Ps. 9:10 GW).

Lord, I want to know You for who You really are. I desire to trust and follow You more and more each day. In Jesus' name, Amen.

When I say: I am afraid to trust God.

God **says:** Spend time with Me and get to know My heart by depending on Me a little more each day.

Those who know your name trust you, O
Lord, because you have never deserted those
who seek your help. (Ps. 9:10 GW)

6

From Wimp to Warrior

*For God has not given us a spirit of fear and timidity, but
of power, love, and self-discipline.*

2 Timothy 1:7 NLT

---

*W*hen Gideon destroyed Baal's altar as God instructed him
to do, the Midianites found out and were furious! They
gathered a force of 135,000 men and prepared for battle. Then
"the Spirit of the LORD came on Gideon" and he took his first
step of faith (Judg. 6:34). He blew a trumpet, summoning allies
to follow him, and sent messengers throughout the region, calling
his people to arms.

But suddenly something changed, and Gideon's fear returned.

Gideon asked if he could place a wool fleece on the threshing
floor and for God to confirm His promise to save Israel by Gideon's
hand by putting the morning dew only on the fleece and leaving
the ground around it dry. Then Gideon would know God would
keep His promise.

And that is what happened. Gideon rose early the next day; he squeezed the fleece and wrung out the dew—a bowlful of water. But that wasn't enough.

> Then Gideon said to God, "Do not be angry with me. Let me make just one more request. Allow me one more test with the fleece, but this time make the fleece dry and let the ground be covered with dew." That night God did so. Only the fleece was dry; all the ground was covered with dew. (vv. 39–40)

I love Gideon because he's a lot like me. He's got such a back-and-forth faith. He longs for more assurance but he's also afraid God is going to be mad at him for asking for it. And I know just how he feels. I want to be confident forever and never struggle with doubt or fear again. But I'm human.

Still, many times I'm concerned that God is as frustrated with me as I am. Then God shows me His amazing grace and patience in stories like Gideon's. He reminds me that faith is not about my performance but rather my dependence on Him.

Gideon was afraid, but what mattered most is that he asked God to give him courage instead of trying to drum it up on his own. So what did God do next? Well, He didn't want to risk the Israelites taking credit for the victory He was going to give them, so He told Gideon:

> "You have too many men. I cannot deliver Midian into their hands, or Israel would boast against me, 'My own strength has saved me.' Now announce to the army, 'Anyone who trembles with fear may turn back and leave Mount Gilead.'" So twenty-two thousand men left, while ten thousand remained. (7:2–3)

There were still too many men, so God pared them down again and Gideon ended up with only three hundred men. God told Gideon He would save him and give the Midianites into his hands with the help of these three hundred.

During that night the LORD said to Gideon, "Get up, go down against the camp, because I am going to give it into your hands. If you are afraid to attack, go down to the camp with your servant Purah and listen to what they are saying. Afterward, you will be encouraged to attack the camp." (vv. 9–11)

So did Gideon take advantage of God's "if you are afraid" clause? You bet he did! He and Purah went down to the enemy's camp, where they heard a man talking about his dream and how the Midianites were growing afraid of Gideon and his army (vv. 13–14).

When Gideon heard the dream and its interpretation, he bowed down and worshiped. He returned to the camp of Israel and called out, "Get up! The LORD has given the Midianite camp into your hands. . . . Watch me," he told them. "Follow my lead. When I get to the edge of the camp, do exactly as I do." (vv. 15, 17)

Can you hear the confidence in Gideon's voice? This was a man who had lived in fear, but now he was leading with courage!

Gideon's three hundred men followed his lead, doing everything he said to do. While they stood in their positions around the camp, every one of the thousands of Midianites ran, crying out as they fled. God caused them to turn on each other with their swords.

The odds may have been against Gideon, but God was for him! By seeking to know and choosing to trust in his promise-keeping Lord, a wimp became a warrior.

When I say: I'm afraid to do what God is calling me to do.

God **says:** I have not given you a spirit of fear.

For God has not given us a spirit of fear and timidity, but of power, love, and self-discipline. (2 Tim. 1:7 NLT)

7

Sometimes I Have to Boss
My Heart Around

Praise the Lord, *my soul; all my inmost being, praise his holy name. Praise the* Lord, *my soul, and forget not all his benefits.*

Psalm 103:1–2

I caught my heart heading to a pit of discouragement for spring break. It was supposed to go to the beach with my family and me, but it was not cooperating.

We had been hit by one emotional and financial crisis after another. A close friend learned that, after a year's worth of abdominal pain, extreme fatigue, and an undiagnosable illness, she had a large tumor that appeared to be ovarian cancer.

That same week our air conditioner broke—again. And a week later, we found out our international adoption expenses could not be applied as a deduction that year, which meant we owed significantly more in taxes than we had anticipated—yet our savings had been poured into our adoption and our air conditioning repairs.

My heart was overwhelmed. My spirit was depleted. And my body was exhausted.

I couldn't stop worrying about my friend. I couldn't stop thinking about our finances. And how was I supposed to relax and enjoy spring break with all we had going on?

Although I had packed my bags for the beach, my heart had decided it wasn't in the mood for vacation. It was marching straight toward the pit.

But as much as I didn't want to go on vacation, I knew I didn't want to dwell in a place of despair or pull my family in with me. It was not part of God's plans—nor mine. Somebody had to take charge of my emotions, so I decided it was time to boss my heart around!

King David was really good at getting bossy by telling his heart and soul what to do. In Psalm 103 he said: "Praise the LORD, my soul; all my inmost being, praise his holy name" (v. 1).

I decided to follow his example. In the midst of my turmoil and troubles, I told my soul to praise the Lord. Now this wasn't a superficial "say your bedtime prayers" talk to my soul. No, this was a deep-down, preach it to my inmost being, "GOD IS GOOD no matter what your feelings are telling you" sermon. I bossed my heart with truth and pulled it away from the pit by telling myself to "forget not ALL his benefits" (v. 2).

I walked my heart down memory lane, reminding myself of the goodness of Him who:

- forgives all my sins and heals all my diseases
- redeems my life from the pit
- crowns me with love and compassion
- satisfies my desires with good things
- renews my youth like the eagle's (vv. 3–5)

No matter what the answer was to my friend's diagnosis, or how costly our air conditioner was going to be, or how much we owed in taxes, my soul needed to praise the Lord. My heart needed to . . .

Remember who God is.

Thank God for what He had done in the past.

Trust God for what He would do in the future.

My circumstances didn't change, but my perspective did. By redirecting my thoughts and my focus, I was able to redirect my emotions. And our spring break wasn't ruined after all.

Are there circumstances that have pulled you into a place of discouragement? Do you have concerns that are causing your thoughts to head down a path of despair? I pray you won't go there.

Every time you are tempted to start worrying about what might be, use King David's prayer to focus on what was, is, and will forever be: God's faithfulness to walk by your side and navigate your heart through the valleys of life.

You can be in charge of your emotions by telling your heart what to do—and if you have to get a little bossy, that's okay too!

Dear Lord, please help me trust You. Empower me through Your Spirit to stop my emotions from bossing me around. I want to quit worrying about what might happen and focus on what has already happened by remembering and praising You for Your faithfulness in my life. In Jesus' name, Amen.

When I say: Everything is going wrong in my life.

God **says:** Focus on Me instead of your circumstances, and remember how I've taken care of you before.

> Praise the LORD, my soul; all my inmost being,
> praise his holy name. Praise the LORD, my soul,
> and forget not all his benefits. (Ps. 103:1–2)

8

Becoming the Woman
God Created You to Be

But in fact God has placed the parts in the body, every one of them, just as he wanted them to be. If they were all one part, where would the body be? As it is, there are many parts, but one body.

1 *Corinthians 12:18–20*

I'm pretty sure it started in middle school. I *really* didn't like who I was, but I wanted everyone else to like me. When I was in sixth grade we moved to a small town in North Carolina. During the first few weeks of school I got teased for my freckles, my fair skin, and my weird accent.

Although I couldn't change how I looked or talked, I could change what I liked and how I acted. My strategy was simple. I compared myself to girls around me and tried to figure out who was most popular, so I could be like them.

Unfortunately it took me decades to break free from constant comparison. How about you?

The saddest thing about our tendency to compare ourselves with one another is that it makes us compete with each other. Yet God never intended for us to compete. He wants us to *complete* one another—encouraging each other's strengths while discovering and embracing our own so we can become who He created us to be.

The apostle Paul explains why in Ephesians 2:10, "For [you] are God's handiwork, created in Christ Jesus to do good works, which God prepared in advance for [you] to do."

The only way we'll break free from the comparison trap is by embracing who we are instead of trying to be who we're not. So how do we start? First, trust that God made you just as He wanted you to be, and then be the best YOU. Discover and offer the unique personality traits God gave you to impact those around you.

Your personality is your natural way of doing things and relating to others. You have strengths and what I call "relational challenges" that God intentionally wove together when He was making you.

Some of us are people-oriented and sensitive to others' feelings, while some of us are more task-oriented and feel less empathy. He created those who love to talk and live life on the fly, and others who love to listen and schedule plans in advance. Although all of us are different, we each bring something valuable to our circumstances and relationships.

It wasn't until I was in my thirties, feeling miserable, that I realized I was still stuck in the comparison trap: I was serving where I was needed but not where I was gifted, and I was trying to find my purpose yet felt confused because I still didn't really like who I was.

In her book *Personality Plus*, Florence Littauer describes four personality types.[1] This book helped me discover and value the unique way God made me. But when I read all of the traits in it for the first time, I felt like I had multiple personalities! In actuality, most of us are a unique blend of two of these personality types.

I have included a summary of these four personalities in appendix A for you to use to help you identify which personality traits best describe you. Take a moment now, or plan a time in the near future, to write a prayer of commitment to get to know the woman God designed you to be. Study the personality types to see which one or two strike a chord in you.

By identifying and embracing my unique personality traits, abilities, and gifts, I found freedom from the comparison trap. And you can too!

Let's be women who no longer compare and compete but rather celebrate and complete our friendships, churches, workplaces, and homes with the unique offerings we bring. You'll love the freedom and confidence that comes when you become the woman God created you to be!

Dear Lord, thank You that I'm Your masterpiece, created anew in Christ Jesus so I can do the good things You planned for me long ago. I want to stop comparing myself with others so I can become who You created me to be. In Jesus' name, Amen.

When I say: I don't like who I am or how I do things.

God **says:** I made you and love you just the way you are!

For [you] are God's handiwork, created in Christ Jesus to do good works, which God prepared in advance for [you] to do. (Eph. 2:10)

9

Because God's Love Is Perfect

Being confident of this, that he who began a good work in you will carry it on to completion until the day of Christ Jesus.

Philippians 1:6

The more we scraped the wood on our windowsills, the more the paint peeled. What we thought would take hours turned into days.

Earlier that week, our neighborhood architectural committee had left a notice on our front door, announcing that we needed to paint our windowsills and front porch columns within thirty days or we'd be fined.

I was humiliated and very frustrated! We'd just completed kitchen renovations and installed new flooring throughout our house, and now this?

My humiliation turned to ranting when my husband got home. "There are four hundred houses in our neighborhood and plenty are in worse condition," I said. "And how could they see our windowsills? We have large trees in our yard that block the view from the street. They must have come onto our property!"

I marched to the curb to prove my point and, from a distance, our house looked fine. However, as I got closer I noticed the paint had worn thin and did indeed need repair.

That day, as I painted, I realized I was no longer mad at our neighborhood committee. Instead, I was glad someone cared enough to notice and tell us.

So it is with Jesus. He notices and cares enough to tell us our hearts need repair. He won't leave a warning on our front door, but He did leave Himself as a love letter nailed to the cross of Calvary, declaring the depth of His love for us. Through His death and resurrection, He offers to repair the peeling paint in our hearts and the rotting wood in our lives.

When we respond to God's invitation and accept Jesus' gift of salvation, we don't just accept a new philosophy of life. We establish a personal relationship with our Creator, the One who knows us and accepts us fully but who also desires our transformation so we can become all He created us to be.

The only way we'll have a confident heart is if we move beyond knowing about God to knowing and relying on Him—to depending on His Word with our heart, mind, and soul.

Maybe, like me, you have believed in Him for years—but you haven't really *believed* Him completely. At least you don't always feel or live like His promises are true for you. Maybe you know God loves you and forgives you, but you still beat yourself up for the ways you've let Him and others down.

Today can be the day the gospel of grace moves from your head to your heart. Today can be the day you step out of the shadows of doubt and start really living in the truth.

Will you let your desire to be known and loved just as you are lead you into a more personal and intimate relationship with Jesus? The first step is to embrace your imperfections in the light of God's perfect love, "being confident of this, that he who began a good work in you will carry it on to completion until the day of Christ Jesus" (Phil. 1:6).

Or maybe you know about God but you don't personally know God. If you would like to accept Jesus as Lord of your life, you can pray the following prayer or use it as a guide to create your own. Just talk to God from your heart, with honesty and sincerity.

Lord, I am sorry I have done things to separate myself from You and other people. I know I have sinned against You and today I receive Your gift of forgiveness. I could never earn salvation by good works, but I put my trust in what Jesus did for me on the cross when He died and rose again. Come into my heart and be Lord of my life. I trust You and thank You for loving me so much. In Jesus' name, Amen.

Wherever you are, Jesus meets you there. You and I are not worthy of His love and we can never do anything to deserve it—but we are worth His love because He chose to give it to us. Hold on to this promise and live in the power of its truth: *because God's love is perfect, you don't have to be!*

———

Jesus, thank you for noticing and caring enough to tell me when my heart needs repair. Thank you for becoming a love letter nailed to the cross of Calvary, declaring the depth of Your love for me. In Your name I pray, Amen.

When I say: I feel so flawed and imperfect.

God **says:** Because My love for you is perfect, you don't have to be.

> Being confident of this, that he who began a good work in you will carry it on to completion until the day of Christ Jesus. (Phil. 1:6)

10

How Are You, Really?

"My grace is sufficient for you, for power is perfected in weakness." Most gladly, therefore, I will rather boast about my weaknesses, so that the power of Christ may dwell in me.

2 Corinthians 12:9 NASB

How hard is it for you to let people know how you're doing? I mean how you're *really* doing.

I think most of us tend to keep our guard up and shy away from letting others in. Yet don't we long to let our guard down and depend on others, especially when we're in need of help, prayer, and encouragement?

Sometimes we tell people we're fine even when we're not, because we want to be. Or we hope that by saying we are fine, eventually we will be. Other times we act like we're fine because others expect us to be. And then there are days when hormones trump all good manners and everyone within ten feet knows you are *not* fine. In fact, what you really meant, in code, is that you are Frazzled, Irritated, Neurotic, and Exhausted!

Recently, my friend Melanie shared about her struggle to be real on her blog. I was so moved by her transparency and perspective that I asked if I could share it with you:

She walks the hallway, fighting back tears threatening to well up again. It's been a long week, filled with betrayal and disappointment. Her future is uncertain. Back at the office, she tries to maintain normalcy. When eyes meet, she is faced with another routine, "How are you?"

"*I'm fine*," she answers, with a plastic smile that hides her pain.

. . . Across town, a young father shakes hands with his fourth interviewer that month. "Thank you for your time," he says. On the way home, his wife calls to see if there's any hope he'll get the job. They have mouths to feed, a car on its last miles . . . "*It will be fine*," he assures her. As he hangs up, his head hangs in despair.

. . . A single mom sits on the park bench, holding her baby close, surrounded by happy couples with smiling children. She never expected to raise a child alone. The pain is sometimes too much to bear. Will she ever feel like she belongs? That she is wanted? Loved? Beautiful?

"*We will be fine*," she whispers into her baby's tiny ear.

"*I'm fine* . . ."

"*We're fine* . . ."

"*Doing great* . . ."

Or are we?

Could we take off the mask that we live the "fairy tale," especially as Christians? We are certainly blessed, in every circumstance guarded by the Father, but honestly, in the deepest parts, sometimes we aren't fine.

I'm not fine. If I took off my mask, would you think less of me, or would you think I'm . . . human?

We don't have it all under control, and I can't help but think that when we act like we do, we basically tell God we don't need Him. *We've got this.*

By pretending we're "fine" we tell others something must be wrong with them if they are hurting . . . because *we* certainly are *not* hurting. *We're fine.*

What if we let someone else in? What if we said, "I'm hurting, and the details aren't important, but would you please pray for me? I would really appreciate that." Could that help them, in return, reach out when they are hurting?

Let's grant one another permission to not be fine as we come broken before the Father, and cry out for His mercy and strength. He did promise to never leave us nor forsake us. Even when we don't feel it, could we still cling to His promise and claim it? *He knows we're not fine.*

Could trials be the very things that break the strings holding on our mask, allowing it to fall to the ground so we cling to Him a little tighter?

The truth is . . .

We aren't fine . . . *We are forgiven.*

We aren't in control . . . *We are held by the hands that control our very heartbeat.*

We aren't invincible . . . *We are made to look to the only One who can heal the broken.*[1]

Jesus, I need courage to cut the strings that hold my mask on and to be real about how I'm really doing with just one other person this week. Show me who needs to see the battle wounds and scars I carry in order for them to stop pretending too. In Your name, Amen.

When I say: I'm fine (although I'm really not).

God **says:** You don't have to pretend. My power is perfected in your weakness, and others want to know you are not perfect.

> "My grace is sufficient for you, for power is per-
> fected in weakness." Most gladly, therefore, I will
> rather boast about my weaknesses, so that the power
> of Christ may dwell in me. (2 Cor. 12:9 NASB)

11

When Your Feelings
Don't Tell the Truth

*We do not belong to those who shrink back and are de-
stroyed, but to those who have faith and are saved.*

Hebrews 10:39

"Things will never change."
"My life isn't going to get better."
"I'll never have the confidence I need."

There are times when I feel paralyzed by thoughts like these. Times
when deep discouragement laces my emotions with uncertainty.

Times when I let Satan convince me that my feelings of defeat
and discouragement are normal.

Times when I shrink back from changes and challenges, as well
as opportunities and open doors. There have also been times when
I've pulled back in my relationships—with family, friends, and
even God. Shrinking back into a place of unbelief . . . settling for
less than God's best.

All because I was tired of muddling through apprehension and indecision.

Has doubt convinced you that feeling inadequate and discouraged is normal? Or that having confident assurance isn't possible for someone like you? I think we sometimes forget we have an adversary who uses self-doubt against us—an opponent who shouts from the sidelines:

"You might as well quit."

"Go ahead and give up."

"You don't have what it takes."

Today you can take a stand and stop listening to the lies. God wants you to know and believe that with Christ *all things* are possible—even you having a confident heart that lives with lasting assurance in Him.

Otherwise doubt, and your enemy, will win every time and your heart will be eroded by attitudes and emotions of defeat.

But it's not supposed to be this way. All throughout Scripture, God tells us things can change; life can be better. He declares with confidence:

See, I am doing a new thing! (Isa. 43:19)
I am working all things together for good for those who love me and are called according to my purpose. (Rom. 8:28)
All things are possible to [her] who believes. (Mark 9:23)

What if we stopped listening to our hearts when our feelings don't tell us the truth and instead we chose to believe God's words more than our fears and doubts?

Let's map out our thoughts and walk in the power of God's Word today—living like it is true—no matter what our feelings tell us.

It will be a moment-by-moment, doubt-by-doubt decision. Will you commit to process your thoughts and emotions with God, positioning your heart and mind to let His perspective redefine yours with each uncertainty you face?

With God's help it's possible to have lasting Christ-confidence by choosing to remember to believe Him. Choose to remember today's truth, in this moment and the next, because you are not a woman who shrinks back and is destroyed—but a woman who believes and is saved!

Lord, give me a confident heart in Christ. I want You to lead me beyond believing in You to truly believing You. Help me rely on the power of Your promises and live like they are true. In Jesus' name, Amen.

When I say: I just want to quit.

God **says:** Don't give in and let discouragement win.

> [You] do not belong to those who shrink
> back and are destroyed, but to those who
> have faith and are saved. (Heb. 10:39)

12

Sin Doesn't Get the Final Say

Therefore, there is now no condemnation for those who are in Christ Jesus.

Romans 8:1

---

*S*he never thought anyone would find out about their affair, but now her secret and her sin would be public.

Just as the people gathered in the temple, surrounding Jesus as He sat down to teach them, the teachers of the law and the Pharisees brought in a woman who had been caught in the act of adultery.

> They made her stand before the group and said to Jesus, "Teacher, this woman was caught in the act of adultery. In the Law Moses commanded us to stone such women. Now what do you say?" They were using this question as a trap, in order to have a basis for accusing him. (John 8:3–6)

They hoped Jesus would condemn her, but the opposite happened. Instead of lording over her, Jesus lowered Himself to His knees before her, bending down to write on the ground.

But Jesus bent down and started to write on the ground with his finger. When they kept on questioning him, he straightened up and said to them, "Let any one of you who is without sin be the first to throw a stone at her." Again he stooped down and wrote on the ground. (vv. 6–8)

The Bible doesn't say what He wrote. Yet I have often wondered if He wrote the Ten Commandments, since her accusers mentioned that Moses' law commanded them to stone her. And, when He was finished writing, Jesus challenged them to examine their own sins and see if any of them were without fault.

Then Jesus stooped down again to write a second time. Again we don't know what He chose to write in the dirt, but perhaps Jesus wrote redemptive words like grace, forgiveness, and mercy. Whatever He wrote, something radical happened. Everyone dropped their stones and walked away.

At this, those who heard began to go away one at a time, the older ones first, until only Jesus was left, with the woman still standing there. Jesus straightened up and asked her, "Woman, where are they? Has no one condemned you?"

"No one, sir," she said.

"Then neither do I condemn you," Jesus declared. "Go now and leave your life of sin." (vv. 9–11)

In the presence of Jesus, the woman's accusers went away. He dismissed them one by one, until He was the only one left standing. Her sin didn't get the final say; Jesus did.

Although He knew she had sinned, Jesus knew her sin was not *who* she was. It was what she had done.

When Jesus stooped down, He helped this woman stand up and find freedom in the promise that "there is now no condemnation for those who are in Christ Jesus" (Rom. 8:1).

The next time condemnation sweeps across your thoughts with statements such as *You're a failure* or *You can never be counted on*,

I hope you will recognize that as the accuser. His tone is condemning, questioning, and confusing. His accusations lead to shame.

Jesus' conviction will be loving and specific. He will reveal a sinful action or attitude and show us what we need to do to right our wrong.

- Instead of *You're such a failure as a [wife, mom, daughter, friend]*, the Spirit might say: *You were critical in the way you talked to _____. You need to say you are sorry and ask forgiveness. Then tell them something to build them up.*
- Instead of *You can never be counted on*, the Spirit might say: *You didn't keep your promise to visit your mom today. Call to apologize and set up a time to meet this weekend.*

Remember, Jesus will never condemn us, but He will lovingly convict us. He invites us out of darkness by leading our hearts to repentance. His desire is to draw us away from destructive behaviors that hinder our relationship with Him and others, so we can live in the freedom of His forgiveness and the security of His love.

Lord, You say there is no condemnation for those who are in Christ Jesus, and my life is hidden in You. Thank You that because of Your love and grace, my sin never gets the final say about me—You do! In Jesus' name, Amen.

When I say: I feel so ashamed and condemned.

God **says:** Shame is from the evil one. I will never condemn you.

Therefore, there is now no condemnation for those who are in Christ Jesus. (Rom. 8:1)

13

When You Don't Want to Be a Burden

Never stop praying, especially for others. Always pray by the power of the Spirit. Stay alert and keep praying for God's people.

Ephesians 6:18 CEV

---

*A*lthough my email was intended to be a prayer request, it started out more like an apology. I needed friends to pray, but I was hesitant to ask them. I didn't want my burdens to burden them. After all, the group of friends I was sending the email to already had so many problems of their own: illness, job loss, death, stress, relationship strains, overloaded schedules.

I wondered if my need rated high enough on the urgency "Richter scale." Was it bad enough to ask for prayer, or should I wait to see how things turned out?

The first sentence in my email went something like this: "I hate to add to your list of burdens, but I need prayer for JJ."

My husband JJ's doctor had expressed concerns about his liver and wanted to do a biopsy that week. I didn't know whether it was going to be anything serious in the end. I just knew that I didn't want to walk through it in fear, in denial, or in my own strength.

I didn't want to go through it alone either. I wanted my man to have as much spiritual protection as possible. I wanted those doctors to be anointed in prayer, and I knew if girlfriends were praying, things would be okay.

Within fifteen minutes of my hitting "send," friends who were on their computers started telling me they were praying. And not only did they pray, they thanked me for sharing what was going on and for letting them be there for me. One friend shared how someone she knew had been through a similar situation. Another asked questions and made some great suggestions. Then another cracked a funny joke that made me laugh, which I really needed to do!

The night before we went to the hospital, I got an email from my friend Amy that read, "I've been lifting prayers heavenward for your family since your last email. Know that you'll be in my thoughts and prayers tomorrow. Let us know as soon as you hear results. We're all in this with you, friend."

As I read her last sentence, it was as though I could feel the softness of her hands gently squeeze my shoulders and hear her voice saying, "We're all in this with you, friend."

What if I had not shared our need? I would've missed out on the comfort of having them "with me" and the peace that came as a result of their prayers. They would've missed out on the opportunity to be the "body of Christ" by guarding our hearts and minds with God's promises and the power of prayer. And they would have missed the joy of celebrating medical tests that went well, peace that surpassed our understanding, and recovery that was quick. Even as we waited for test results, their prayers and God's peace were our constant companions.

When you are carrying a heavy burden, don't listen to doubts that make you question the validity of your need. Even if you're like me and hate to impose on others.

God wants us to remember that asking for prayer isn't about putting burdens on our friends. It's about letting them walk by our side down a path we were never intended to walk alone. In return, they will invite you to do the same.

Lord, thank You for never seeing my prayers as a burden. Please teach me more about the power and the purpose of prayer in my life and in my friendships. In Jesus' name, Amen.

When I say: I don't want to be a burden on others.

God **says:** Let those close to you encourage you, pray for you, and comfort you in times of need.

Never stop praying, especially for others. Always
pray by the power of the Spirit. Stay alert and keep
praying for God's people. (Eph. 6:18 CEV)

14

I Haven't Got Time for the Pain

The LORD will surely comfort [you] and will look with compassion on all [your] ruins; he will make [your] deserts like Eden, [your] wastelands like the garden of the LORD.

Isaiah 51:3

I needed to talk about the pain that was buried in my heart, but I didn't want to. I was tired of hurting and afraid I'd fall apart if I let it come to the surface. I didn't have time to fall apart and thought it would just go away.

Have you ever avoided dealing with pain because it would take too much time? Or have you tried to pray away the pain only to realize healing is a process?

Although we can't go back and change circumstances or relationships that wounded us, we can go back and process our pain with Jesus. Otherwise, the pain from our yesterdays can creep up on our todays and keep us from experiencing all God has for our tomorrows.

This happened in my relationship with my husband several years into our marriage. I didn't know why, but I felt angry and critical toward JJ. When I finally asked God for help, He showed me damaged emotions from my childhood I hadn't dealt with or healed from.

I decided to take time to look back so I could move forward. I asked the Holy Spirit to remind me of things that had wounded me, and the effect they had on me.

God showed me how years of disappointment as a child in a broken home with a broken heart had led to a significant sense of loss. Yet I had never grieved the happily-ever-after I longed for but didn't have. Unfulfilled hopes had led to bitter expectations.

I wanted JJ to make up for what my dad had never been as a father to me or as a husband to my mom. Hoping to create my own version of "happily-ever-after," I became controlling and critical. But my strategy wasn't working.

With each revelation, I took time to process it in prayer with Jesus so I could heal from the pain of my past and deal with my disappointments—but not dwell in them either.

I also took time to seek God for my security and hope by letting Him be the father I longed for. And I gave myself some time to grieve and let go of what I wanted from my father that I would never have. I invited God into my hurting places so He could heal my wounded emotions and set me free from my fear of never having a happy ending.

Finally, I forgave my father and released my feelings of anger, abandonment, disappointment, and hurt. I also confessed my sin of unrealistic expectations and let go of what I thought was my right to "happily-ever-after."

Throughout the whole process, I claimed the comfort and confidence of God's promise in Isaiah 51:3: "The LORD will surely comfort [you] and will look with compassion on all [your] ruins; he will make [your] deserts like Eden, [your] wastelands like the garden of the LORD."

When we allow Jesus to search our hearts and bring His perspective into our pain, redemption comes. Whether it is the pain from our yesterdays or hurts from our todays, when we give Jesus time to pour His truth into our wounds, His love flows into our pain and makes us whole again.

Lord, give me courage and show me how important it is to take time to walk through the process of letting You heal my hurts and restore my heart with hope. I want all that You have for me—it is for freedom You have set me free! In Jesus' name, Amen.

When I say: I haven't got time to deal with my pain.

God **says:** If you don't process the pain from your yesterdays, it will creep into your todays and keep you from experiencing all I have for your tomorrows.

> The LORD will surely comfort [you] and will
> look with compassion on all [your] ruins; he
> will make [your] deserts like Eden, [your] waste-
> lands like the garden of the LORD. (Isa. 51:3)

15

It's Over

My beloved spoke and said to me, "Arise, my darling, my beautiful one, come with me. See! The winter is past; the rains are over and gone."

Song of Songs 2:10–11

---

*T*he lyrics caught in her throat the first time she sang them: "I'll never know how much it cost to see my sin upon the cross."[1]

Samantha cried as she stared at her circumstances, ashamed. She had compromised in some big areas and, until the truth of that song caught her off guard, she had turned a cold shoulder to the hope of forgiveness. Shame convinced her she wasn't worthy of another chance. She remembered the day redemption had come for her as she offered it to others in need while serving with a missions team on the streets of skid row. God reminded her we all need a second chance, she just as much as any other. Here's the story Samantha shared:

It was a 75-degree, gorgeous-in-every-way LA day and there I was, navigating my way around pain and hypodermic needles. And there she was, fidgeting outside the women's shelter.

She melded into the gray of her tattered sweatpants. Washed out and muted, buried under the debris of a dark world, away from the Light for too long. Inching toward me, she stepped over others hibernating beneath cardboard boxes and frigid despair.

Try as I might, I couldn't catch her eyes as she asked for help. Shame from past deeds had beaten her down. It made her doubt she was worthy of anything, much less another chance for a hot meal and cold drink.

This timid woman had been pushed out of the food line. Unable to defend herself and in too much physical pain to stand in line again, she needed someone to make a way for her.

Together, we walked to the front of the food truck (not gonna lie, it was fun breezing past her bullies). But I felt helpless handing her only scrambled eggs and water. Surely, she needed so much more.

We all need more at some point, don't we?

This frail woman needed to know God had more for her than this. That what she'd done to land on skid row could be forgiven—forgotten, even. This cold season could turn into a warmer one. I wanted to share this truth: *"See! The winter is past; the rains are over and gone" (Song of Songs 2:11).*

Winter, that gloomy season that should pass. But what if it lingers? What if one bad-for-us choice turns into 100 that beat us to our own Skid Row? What if mistakes convince us we don't deserve another shot?

Haven't we all been there? But letting the Light of truth into our hearts turns our winter of doubt into a spring of hope.

What we've done doesn't dictate who we are. The truth is, what *He's* done makes us who we are: forgiven, hopeful, and worthy of another chance.

We may not believe we deserve a second shot. But Christ's sacrifice on the cross and our gift of a new life through His death gives us one. When we ask for forgiveness and turn from our sins, our past is covered by God's mercy and grace.

Never doubt, He'll always lead us past the bully of shame to the front of the line for so much more than eggs and water.[2]

God, it's hard to believe I'm worthy of another chance. But I'm taking a step of faith, choosing to accept that Your death means a new life for me. I'll never know how much it cost, but I'm forever grateful. In Jesus' name, Amen.

When I say: I don't deserve another chance.

God **says:** I will remember your sins no more.

For I will be merciful to [your] iniquities, and I will remember [your] sins no more. (Heb. 8:12 NASB)

16

Praying with Confidence

This is the confidence which we have before Him, that, if we ask anything according to His will, He hears us.

1 John 5:14 NASB

I used to be hesitant to pray and stumbled over my words when talking to God. I especially didn't know how to pray when struggling with uncertainty and doubts.

Desperately wanting to say the right things, I believed if I prayed the right way God would listen and answer my prayers the way I wanted Him to.

It took me awhile, but I finally got up the courage to talk with a friend about my fears and struggles. She explained that prayer isn't about saying or asking the right things, it's about building a relationship with God by talking to Him—and listening.

She also taught me how to take Scriptures from the Bible and turn them into powerful prayers. Using God's Word as a guide gave me a new sense of confidence and direction when I didn't know what to say.

One day I was reading 1 John 5:14 and noticed how the Bible says we can pray with certainty when we ask God for what is already part of His will: "This is the confidence which we have before Him, that, if we ask anything according to His will, He hears us" (NASB).

Praying Scriptures increased my confidence over time, knowing that I was praying God's will when I prayed God's Word.

Wanting my prayers to be filled with power and my heart to be infused with faith, I now look for Scriptures about God's will and God's ways. One is Hebrews 4:12, where the Bible teaches us that God's Word is "alive and active." Praying that truth, I ask God to make His Word come alive in a situation and become active in the person's life I am praying for, including my own.

Oftentimes when I pray now, verses that I've read in the Bible will come to mind. For instance, when I feel like my plans are falling apart, Jeremiah 29:11 will pop into my thoughts. On those days, I'll pray:

> *Lord, You know the plans You have for me, plans to prosper me and not to harm me, plans to give me a future and a hope. You say that if I come to You and pray, You will listen and You will lead me. So today I surrender my plans for Your plans. Please guide my decisions and thoughts to match Yours so that I can experience hope and not harm. Even though things aren't going so great today, I trust the plans You have for me.*

God's not looking for the perfect combination of words, and there is no formula to get it right. Now that the pressure to say the right things is gone, prayer has become one of my favorite things to do—whether alone or with a friend.

Sometimes I just sit still and let God whisper His promises into my thoughts, and then I ask for their fulfillment in my prayers.

Lord, I'm so glad I don't have to say the right things to get Your attention. Thank You for Your Spirit who lives in me and leads me—in my daily activities and even in my prayers. Please show me verses You want me to pray today so I can see Your Word come alive in my circumstances and become active in my life. In Jesus' name, Amen.

When I say: I don't know what to say when I pray.

God **says:** Just talk to Me and pray through My promises today.

> This is the confidence which we have be-
> fore Him, that, if we ask anything according to
> His will, He hears us. (1 John 5:14 NASB)

61

17

Away from the Crowds

*But [Jesus] would go away to places where he could be
alone for prayer.*

Luke 5:16 GW

---

*B*efore He chose the twelve disciples, Jesus pulled away
from the crowds and went to a mountain to spend the
night in prayer. After He fed the five thousand, He withdrew to
be alone with God. All throughout His life, Jesus withdrew to be
alone with the Father, all the while teaching His disciples and us
to do the same.

Spending time alone with God is essential to the health of our
heart and mind. It allows our thoughts to get quiet so we can hear
His. But it's not easy in a culture of constant contact, social media,
cell phones, and instant everything.

So how do we find time to spend with Jesus? First, we have to
be honest. We won't *find* time; we have to choose time. And it's
not easy with so many demands and people pulling at us. But there
are a few things that help me.

I plan a d.a.t.e. Just like any other relationship we value, we have to be intentional and plan time to be with Jesus. We won't find ourselves on the couch reading our Bible because we want to. But we can choose to plan a **d.a.t.e.** by determining a time every day to spend with Jesus.

I set realistic expectations. If I have a full day coming, I set aside fifteen to thirty minutes to focus on Jesus, time spent without thinking about who I need to pick up or where I need to be. I do shorter morning devotions and more extensive study of God's Word once or twice a week.

I read my Bible and write down what God shows me. It's imperative that I take my thoughts captive and listen to God's truth over Satan's lies, but I won't know what is true if I haven't spent time with God and recorded truths He's shown me.

I reflect on God's faithfulness. I write thoughts and prayers in my journal so I can remember what God has done. Many times I won't recall what I prayed for, but when I look back over what I've written I see how God has answered. When I find myself in a struggle, I remember God's faithfulness by reflecting on how He has come through again and again.

I get creative. I used to think being a godly woman meant getting up early every morning to pray and read my Bible. But my brain doesn't process thoughts or words early in the morning, so I'd spend that time "guilting" myself for being distracted and groggy. Then one day God whispered to my heart: *Renee, I made you. You like variety and you are not a morning person. I created you, so work with Me. Spend time with Me in the beginning of your day, but don't feel like it has to be the same time in the same place every day.*

Some days I go walking and listen to an audio Bible. Other times I bring index cards with verses on them and pray God's promises out loud. Other days I sit and read my Bible and talk with God through prayer.

I have a special place to meet with Jesus. Although I like variety, I also have a "Jesus chair" in my bedroom with a cozy blanket and lamp that makes it feel very inviting. I keep my Bible, journal, pen, small notepad, and Bible study or devotional book in a basket next to my chair so it's all easy to find. If I'm hurrying out the door and don't spend time with Jesus that morning, I picture Him waiting for me to come back. It's a sweet image and reminder for me.

Lord, I am honored that You want to spend time with me! Help me to seek You as much as (or more than) I serve You. I want to slow down so You can give me Your perspective and fill my heart with confidence in Your presence each day. In Jesus' name, Amen.

When I say: My life is too busy. I don't have time to spend with God.

God **says:** Come with Me to a quiet place and get some rest for your heart, mind, and soul.

> Then, because so many people were coming and
> going that they did not even have a chance to eat,
> he said to them, "Come with me by yourselves to
> a quiet place and get some rest." (Mark 6:31)

18

Giving In or Getting Up Again?

The steps of a man are established by the LORD, and He delights in his way. When he falls, he will not be hurled headlong, because the LORD is the One who holds his hand.

Psalm 37:23–24 NASB

I've always admired people who never give in. You know, the ones who don't consider defeat when they blow it.

I can be really hard on myself when I fall short of the woman God calls me to be or the woman I want to be. Like the other day, when I got really upset with my son Joshua and went on a rant about his laundry not being done and his room being a mess.

Soon after, my internal dialogue (that voice in my head that won't let me off the hook) started reminding me of how badly I'd acted and how scarred my son may be from my harsh words.

Perhaps you have blown it recently and let failure knock you down, tie you up with the ropes of regret, and hold you hostage like I have.

When I surveyed women for my book *A Confident Heart*, I discovered that our past failures, and our fear of failing again, are two of the most common things that make us doubt ourselves.

The greatest defeat comes when I allow my shortfalls, sins, or broken relationships to convince me that I might as well give up. But today's key verse teaches us that instead of giving in, Jesus empowers us to *get up* again.

In getting up, we can apologize and ask for forgiveness. In getting up, we can choose to try again with our kids, in our jobs, in our marriages, in our ministries, and in all of our mistakes.

Listen to today's promise in Psalm 37:23–24, and as you read it insert your name in the blanks: "The steps of _____ are established by the LORD, and He delights in _____'s way. When _____ falls, _____ will not be hurled headlong, because the LORD is the One who holds _____'s hand" (NASB).

Failure can actually help you become the confident woman God created you to be, because when you get up again you become stronger and better—when you go to God for help. Defeat might even be the thing that stretches you to do more than you think you can and pushes you to try new ideas or methods when one way doesn't work.

Remember, following Jesus is not about being perfect. It's about accepting our weaknesses and becoming more dependent on His perfect love and power at work in us. And when we depend on Him, we become the confident women we are meant to be, because instead of giving in, we choose to take God's hand and get up again!

Lord, because You say that my steps are established by You, I will believe You delight in me even when I fail or fall. Today, I want to take Your hand and trust Your heart as You pull me back up again and use my failures to help me become the confident woman You created me to be. In Jesus' name, Amen.

When I say: I'm constantly messing up.

God **says:** Your mistakes don't define you, but you can let them refine you.

> The steps of a man are established by the LORD,
> and He delights in his way. When he falls, he will
> not be hurled headlong, because the LORD is the
> One who holds his hand. (Ps. 37:23–24 NASB)

19

How Forgiveness Sets Us Free

*Be completely humble and gentle; be patient, bearing with
one another in love . . . forgiving each other, just as in
Christ God forgave you.*

Ephesians 4:2, 32

I thought I was over the hurt and had moved on. But as I
slipped my thumb under the seal of the invitation to my
ten-year college reunion, it hit me: I had not forgiven her.

During our last semester at school, the harsh tone and accus-
ing anger of a friend had been more than my heart could handle,
especially in the middle of my year-long battle with depression.
A deep sense of sadness and self-doubt that I couldn't explain or
escape had left me feeling depleted.

When she questioned something I had done and expressed
deep frustration toward me, I didn't have the mental or emotional
strength to process her criticism without being pulled into a pit
of condemnation.

I knew if I attended our class reunion I would likely see her and
other friends who had gotten tangled in our mess. And with that

possibility came a flood of memories and emotions that made me feel the same *yuck* I felt the day our friendship ended—the day that pretty much ruined the last few weeks of our senior year.

Holding the envelope in my hand, all that hurt took hold of me again. Instead of simply deciding how to RSVP, I stood at the edge of a pit filled with insecurity that threatened to pull me back in.

After weeks of thinking about the invitation, I finally decided I was tired of living as a prisoner to my hurt. I wanted freedom, the kind of freedom I had come to know in the ten years in-between. The freedom of forgiveness Jesus died to give me.

I spent hours praying and reading my Bible over the next month. Listening to worship music and messages on forgiveness, I asked God to drench me with His perspective and give me His assurance so I could walk into my reunion as a secure child of God.

By the time I arrived, my mind was filled with God's grace and promises. I literally *wanted* to find my old friend and restore our relationship. The confidence that came as I followed God's command to seek and offer forgiveness came as a surprise.

Forgiving those who have hurt us is hard. Often we are afraid to forgive because it might open us to hurt again. Or we're afraid if we bring something up we might unearth bitterness we don't want to deal with, so we just leave it buried.

But anytime we bury a hurt alive, it will keep rising from the dead to disturb us.

God used today's verses to show me how to let forgiveness set me free from the hurt I had buried. "Be completely humble and gentle; be patient, bearing with one another in love . . . forgiving each other, just as in Christ God forgave you" (Eph. 4:2, 32).

Forgiving others in the way this Scripture describes has helped me recognize I need God's grace as much as anyone else. And although pardoning an offense is not easy, it is possible when we follow God's plan of being humble, gentle, and patient, and bear with others.

Forgiveness is a gift we give ourselves when we offer it to others. In doing so, we don't forgive so we can forget. We forgive, as we have been forgiven, so we can move on from the pain of our yesterdays and live in the freedom God has for us today.

Lord, I need Your help in forgiving. Help me process my hurt with You and let go of any bitterness that keeps me from wholeness and hope. Empower me to forgive just as You have forgiven me. In Jesus' name, Amen.

When I say: I can't forgive them.

God **says:** I will help you as you rely on My grace and forgiveness.

Be completely humble and gentle; be patient, bearing with one another in love . . . forgiving each other, just as in Christ God forgave you. (Eph. 4:2, 32)

20

More Than Breadcrumbs

Why spend money on what is not bread, and your labor on what does not satisfy? Listen, listen to me, and eat what is good, and you will delight in the richest of fare. Give ear and come to me; listen, that you may live.

Isaiah 55:2–3

----

*S*itting on the empty beach enjoying the sunrise, Tracie watched a few seagulls flying aimlessly around, looking lost and confused. She wondered why there were so few, considering the flocks that normally swarmed overhead with screeching cries.

She quickly realized the seagulls had no reason to be on the beach, much less be excited or active. There were no people around to generate crumbs. *Funny how they stay at a distance until they think someone has food and then come running, or I should say dive-bombing*, she thought. *No birds will be in sight, but one tiny crumb falls on the sand and suddenly dozens swoop down out of nowhere.*

Memories of hungry seagulls interrupting their family picnics at the beach made Tracie chuckle, until she sensed God whisper: *Sometimes, Tracie, you are just like those seagulls.*

If I had been sitting on the beach with Tracie, God would have told me the same thing. Unfortunately, there are seasons of life when I settle for crumbs and yet God wants to give me His daily bread.

Recently I noticed how days went by where I threw up a quick prayer, thought about a favorite Bible verse, and then dashed into my day. Some days I would go through the motions of driving kids to school, rushing to meetings at work, tackling a never-ending to-do list, and navigating conflict—on crumbs. And on those evenings I was depleted and anxious. Yet I couldn't sleep even though I was exhausted.

Then something big would happen that made me feel insecure, worried, discouraged, and stressed—and I would dive-bomb into God's presence, hoping He would quickly meet my needs. Impatiently, I waited for Him to give me wisdom and a promise to apply to my problem—to toss me more crumbs of encouragement so I could keep going.

Scripture often draws a parallel between food and our spiritual need for God's Word. For instance, in Isaiah 55, God asks, "Why spend money on what is not bread, and your labor on what does not satisfy? Listen, listen to me, and eat what is good, and you will delight in the richest of fare. Give ear and come to me; listen, that you may live" (vv. 2–3).

I spend a lot of money on food, and time on laboring for good things, but none of those things can satisfy the hunger of my soul. What I need is a daily portion of God's presence, so I can listen to Him and eat what is good as I soak in His perspective, His peace, and His purposes for me.

Tracie and I have decided we don't want to settle for breadcrumbs anymore. We know we were created with a spiritual hunger that can only be satisfied by daily bread, so we're giving up the seagull mentality of surviving on mere crumbs.

Let's ask God to give us a hunger that can never be satisfied by anything but Him. A hunger that pains us if we don't get a daily portion of God's wisdom, love, and guidance. A hunger that, when met, replaces our discontentment and stress with peace and satisfaction.

Jesus, I don't want to keep settling for less than You have for me. When I come to You daily for manna, You supply the perspective and peace I need. Give me a desire and hunger that cannot be satisfied by anything but spending time with You in Your Word. In Your name I pray, Amen.

When I say: No matter how much I do or how much I have, I'm never satisfied.

God **says:** Don't spend so much money and time on things that can't satisfy your soul. Let Me give you what your heart needs.

> Why spend money on what is not bread, and your labor on
> what does not satisfy? Listen, listen to me, and eat what is
> good, and you will delight in the richest of fare. Give ear
> and come to me; listen, that you may live. (Isa. 55:2–3)

21

Set Apart

*I knew you before I formed you in your mother's womb.
Before you were born I set you apart and appointed you
as my prophet to the nations.*

Jeremiah 1:5 NLT

---

*W*hat are you good at? Is there something you would love
to do?" When the facilitator of our small group asked
these questions, I had no answer. At the age of thirty-two I didn't
know what I loved to do or what I was good at.

I'd never taken time to think about it. Instead, I had always tried
to do what others wanted, expected, or needed me to do. And I was
pretty good at all three. But honestly, I was fairly miserable too.

And it's no wonder. I had no idea who God created me to be.
If only I had known the promise of Jeremiah 1:5, where God says:
"I knew you before I formed you in your mother's womb. Before
you were born I set you apart" (NLT).

Just like God called and equipped the prophet Jeremiah to be
His mouthpiece to the Israelites, He has a specific call and gifting
for each of us. And He establishes both before we are even born.

After I fumbled for an answer, our facilitator encouraged me to ask God what *He* created me to do and what would give me joy. She helped me see that I wasn't designed to be who others expected me to be, or even wanted me to be.

I was created to become all that God created me to be.

Isn't it easy to neglect ourselves to meet the needs of everyone around us and call it self-sacrifice? It sounds godly. But in doing so we risk shutting down a place in our soul where God has gifted us and set us apart—to serve and thrive.

I took our facilitator's advice and read books that talked about discovering our gifts. I started to identify what I liked. I recognized strengths that came naturally to me, and for the first time I realized there was an important reason God made me who I am.

Do you know what you're good at and what you love to do?

One of the ways we can discover God's unique calling on our lives is through our spiritual gifts. Unlike talents and abilities received at our natural birth, spiritual gifts are received at our spiritual birth. When we accept Jesus as Lord and Savior, God's presence indwells our hearts in the form of the Holy Spirit.

Along with His presence comes a "present," more commonly referred to as a *spiritual gift*. It's thoughtfully chosen by our heavenly Father to help us fulfill His plans for us.

There are three main ways to discover our spiritual gifts. First is through experience in serving. When my pastor, Derwin Gray, was in the NFL, he became a Christian. He knew God wanted him to serve but he wasn't sure how, so he started volunteering in the prayer ministry at his church. One Sunday, his pastor asked him to share his testimony in the service, and that day Derwin discovered his passion and giftedness for teaching God's Word. Today he is the lead pastor of one of the fastest growing multiethnic congregations in the United States—but he didn't start there.

Second, ask someone who knows you and has seen you serving. Friends and leaders in ministry are a great resource to help you find that place in the body of Christ best suited for you and your giftedness.

Finally, ask yourself: *What gives me a sense of joy and fulfillment when I am contributing to ministry or something of spiritual significance?* Then go do it.

Remember, God had a plan in mind when He made you. When you discover and begin to intentionally use your spiritual gifts, God will use them to guide you toward the plans and purposes for which He has set you apart—to fulfill His dreams for your life.

Lord, I want to know the woman You had in mind when You created me. I don't want to grow old and never know Your purpose for my life. Show me the gifts and dreams You have for me, so I can offer what You want to give to others in my life. In Jesus' name, Amen.

When I say: I'm not really good at anything.

God **says:** I have set you apart with unique gifts to equip you for what I've created you to do.

I knew you before I formed you in your mother's womb.
Before you were born I set you apart and appointed
you as my prophet to the nations. (Jer. 1:5 NLT)

22

When Helping Others Helps Us

Have I not commanded you? Be strong and courageous.
Do not be afraid; do not be discouraged, for the LORD *your*
God will be with you wherever you go.

Joshua 1:9

I do not like open heights. I can't stand narrow balconies. And when I'm driving across a bridge, you'll find me hugging the rail along the inside lane.

A few years ago, some friends tried to help me conquer my fear of heights by inviting our family to an indoor rock climbing center. My heart raced as we entered the doors and faced a twenty-five-foot peak. The instructors assured me that a web of ropes and harnesses would hold me tight.

Before I could say "no thank you," I was strapped in and signing an injury waiver.

Toward the end of the day our friends, John and Laura, asked their eight-year-old son Steven if he wanted to climb the highest peak. Steven wasn't crazy about heights, but he loved a challenge.

With admiration I watched as Steven started the climb with confidence. He made it to ten feet, then fifteen, then twenty. But as he inched past the next face of the wall, he looked down. Realizing how high he was and how far he still had to go, he insisted he couldn't do it.

By this time, his dad was consoling their very fussy three-year-old and his mom was feeding their hungry infant daughter. My brave husband was not close by, and I quickly realized I was the only one standing there who had a free hand to do something.

Suddenly courage and strength surged through my body and I called out, "Don't give up, buddy. You can do it. I'll help you!"

In record time, I reached the twenty-foot marker, crossed over, and was up beside Steven to encourage him, reminding him of how far he'd come. I told him he could do it with God's strength and that it would be worth it if he'd persevere.

With my words and confidence in him, Steven turned his eyes and his thoughts toward the reward of getting to a place he had stopped believing he could reach.

And the same was true for me.

The voices of my own fears were silenced by focusing on helping someone overcome theirs.

In that moment, I realized the promises I had claimed for Steven were true for me too. My anxiety could be overcome and my fears conquered with God's strength.

Each day we have the same opportunity. Like God did with Joshua, and like He does with us, we can come alongside each other in some of life's hardest challenges and highest peaks. "Have I not commanded you? Be strong and courageous. Do not be afraid; do not be discouraged, for the LORD your God will be with you wherever you go" (Josh. 1:9). In other words, we can encourage others: "Don't give up, you can do it. I'll be with you and I will help you."

Isn't it amazing that when we take our eyes off our fears, doubts, and struggles to focus on someone else's needs, we somehow forget our own? In believing the power of God's promises for others, our confidence in His promises for us increases.

Let's look for ways to encourage and help someone else today, knowing we may just help ourselves in the process.

Jesus, Your words give me courage to become who You've created me to be—to go to places You're calling me to and to reach heights that seem out of my reach. Thank You for encouraging my heart. Help me pass that on to someone else today. In Your name I pray, Amen.

When I say: Will I ever conquer my fears?

God **says:** I will help you as you help others.

> Have I not commanded you? Be strong and courageous.
> Do not be afraid; do not be discouraged, for the LORD
> your God will be with you wherever you go. (Josh. 1:9)

23

Letting God Rebuild Your Confidence

Such confidence we have through Christ before God. Not that we are competent in ourselves to claim anything for ourselves, but our competence comes from God.

2 Corinthians 3:4–5

As someone ever asked you a question that opened your eyes to something you were struggling with?

My friend Amy and her husband, Barry, were sitting on their deck talking one night, when suddenly Barry asked Amy a startling question. "If you could change one thing about me, what would it be?"

Amy's mind went blank except for the thought, *Whew! This is a really loaded question.* At first she didn't want to answer (why ruin a great evening?), but after finally answering she braced herself and re-asked the question. "What would you change about *me*?"

Barry's response caught her off guard, but it also helped Amy see one of God's difficult works in her life:

I had a pretty good list going in my mind of what I thought he'd say—*I wish you weren't so critical. I wish you wouldn't talk so much. I wish you would cook dinner more often.*

What he actually said surprised me. "I want you to get your confidence back. When I married you, your favorite phrase was, 'I'll do it myself!' I've watched you lose your confidence over the years, and I want you to have it back," he replied.

A move, a couple of friendships with bad endings, and struggles to find a place in my new hometown had knocked the stuffing right out of me. I had fought and lost against my own tendency toward comparison, perfectionism, and an overdeveloped sense of responsibility. Little by little, I became convinced that I *couldn't* and that I *wasn't*. My confidence had been shaken and finally crumbled.

Sometimes things have to be torn down before they can be rebuilt.

Was it God's plan that I would move, fail in some friendships, and beat myself up trying to be somebody else? No.

He did, however, use this really bad place in my life to bring me to a better place. God started rebuilding my confidence in the weeks that followed Barry's surprising question and startling response.

Around that same time my Sunday school class discussed 2 Corinthians 3:4–6: "*Such confidence we have through Christ before God. Not that we are competent in ourselves to claim anything for ourselves, but our competence comes from God. He has made us competent as ministers of a new covenant—not of the letter but of the Spirit; for the letter kills, but the Spirit gives life.*"

As I thought about Barry wanting me to get my confidence back, I remembered my mom asking Barry if he was ready to hold a tiger by the tail when he proposed to me. I had always been a rule-following first-child mixed with a wide streak of sassiness and fierce independence.

Now, over twenty years later, I realized that's because I lived in my own strength of "I can do it," and God was bringing me to His strength, showing me that true confidence comes when I believe "He can do it in me."[1]

God wants to set us free from depending on our own power, which is so inadequate and flawed, so we can be dependent on the power of His Spirit in us.

When relationship failures, job losses, and unexpected life-changes come, our confidence may be shaken—but it doesn't have to crumble. In those times we can ask Jesus to rebuild and renew our sense of confidence firmly in the promise of His power living and working in us.

Confidence in ourselves has very limited potential, but confidence in Christ brings limitless possibilities.

Dear Lord, I depend on myself so many times and I almost always fall short. My confidence has been shaken. Rebuild me by helping me to put my full confidence in You. In Jesus' name, Amen.

When I say: I have no confidence left.

God **says:** I will be your confidence.

For the LORD will be your confidence and will keep
your foot from being caught. (Prov. 3:26 NASB)

24

When Fear Paralyzes Our Faith

Do not fear, for I have redeemed you; I have summoned you by name; you are mine. When you pass through the waters, I will be with you; and when you pass through the rivers, they will not sweep over you. When you walk through the fire, you will not be burned; the flames will not set you ablaze.

Isaiah 43:1–2

Fear can be powerful and paralyzing to our faith. I know because I have been its victim. Fear-infused doubt kept me from enjoying carousel rides as a child, waterskiing as a teen, and trust as a new bride—but that is not all. I accepted my fear as though it were a handicap I was born with, and let fear infect every area of my life.

During my early years of marriage, I was afraid to sleep at night whenever my husband was out of town for work. I knew I needed to trust God, but I didn't. In addition to praying, reading Scriptures, and taping verses to my bedside table and mirror, I slept with my phone, our neighborhood directory, and my Bible.

One night I also put toys on the stairs to trip any burglars, put my children in my room to sleep with me, and put my dresser in front of my bedroom door. I thought I was controlling my circumstances, but instead fear had taken control of me. When I still couldn't sleep, I opened my Bible and read these words:

Do not fear, for I have redeemed you; I have summoned you by name; you are mine. When you pass through the waters, I will be with you; and when you pass through the rivers, they will not sweep over you. When you walk through the fire, you will not be burned; the flames will not set you ablaze. (Isa. 43:1–2)

That night God helped me see that my fears were like flames and my efforts to protect myself like gasoline. Every time I did something, it was like pouring fuel on the fire. My fear was consuming me. God reminded me that He had not given me a spirit of fear but a spirit of power and love and a sound mind (2 Tim. 1:7).

I realized the only way I would overcome my fears was by walking through them. I would have to put away the props I was trusting in, and go to bed trusting God, knowing that even if my fears came true He would be with me. That night I put everything away and walked through the flames of my fear. I did what God was calling me to do, and I slept better than I had in weeks.

Jesus said, "If you hold to my teaching . . . then you will know the truth, and the truth will set you free" (John 8:31–32). Fear loses its power when we actively put our trust in the promises He's given us.

If we want to be free from fear so we can walk in faith, we have to hold on to what God is teaching us, replacing our natural ways with His. We will only overcome our fears by walking through them, holding God's hand, and trusting His heart to lead, protect, and preserve us.

Let's ask God to show us any fears that paralyze our faith and keep us from living confidently in the promises and peace He wants us to have. And then let's give God a chance to come through for us, so we can proclaim like King David, "I sought the LORD, and he answered me; he delivered me from all my fears" (Ps. 34:4).

Dear Jesus, help me trust You with all my heart and lean not on my own understanding. I want to acknowledge You in all my ways so You can make my path straight. Give me courage to face my fears and walk through them with faith as I take hold of all You are teaching me today. In Your name, Amen.

When I say: My fears are paralyzing my faith.

God **says:** Fear not, for I am with you. I have called you by name; you are Mine.

> Do not fear, for I have redeemed you; I have sum-
> moned you by name; you are mine. When you pass
> through the waters, I will be with you; and when you
> pass through the rivers, they will not sweep over you.
> When you walk through the fire, you will not be burned;
> the flames will not set you ablaze. (Isa. 43:1–2)

25

The Things We Do for Love

*"Sir," the woman said, "you have nothing to draw with
and the well is deep. Where can you get this living water?"*

John 4:11

I had almost everything I wanted, yet I felt empty and confused. I couldn't figure out why all the relationships and
accomplishments I had worked so hard to gain weren't enough to
fill me or fulfill me.

Tears streamed down my face as I thought about the guy I had
dated through high school and college. Our plans of a future together had crumbled under the pressure of me expecting him to be
all I needed. I had been crazy about him—a little too crazy.

When I think about the crazy things I did for his love, I want
to crawl under a rock. Like the day a friend mentioned that my
ex-boyfriend was heading to our hometown for the weekend. We
worked near each other, so I parked by his office and waited for
him to leave on Friday.

We both "happened" to be at Wendy's at the same time and
bumped into each other. When I finished my order, I got in my

car and followed behind him, hoping that if he saw my car he'd realize he couldn't live without me and signal for me to pull over so we could talk.

Seriously, what was I thinking? As you can probably guess, he never stopped. I was hopeless and humiliated. Without his love I felt incomplete.

A few weeks later, while walking around my campus one afternoon, my eyes drifted to the buildings, dorms, and other landmarks of memories. Suddenly my mind filled with a collage of faces, reminding me of my efforts to win the approval of advisors, friends, and professors—hoping their affirmation could fill my emptiness.

Although I was graduating with honors, had a few job offers, and had achieved success in many ways, it wasn't enough. I stopped walking and just stood there, taking it all in. I couldn't help but wonder, *Why is all that I have never enough to fill me and fulfill me?*

A thought rushed through my soul, stringing together two words I had never put next to each other, and I sensed God was answering me.

Renee, all you have ever wanted is unconditional love.

Unconditional love? I didn't know there was such a thing. Then I heard another whisper in my soul: *You will never find the love you long for in anyone or anything but Me. I AM the unconditional love you are looking for.*

The thought of God loving me without any conditions was inconceivable, yet something deep in my soul told me it was true. I had been looking for love that didn't have to be earned. Love I didn't have to fear I could lose.

Honestly, though, it took me awhile to see how God's love could fill the emptiness in my heart.

In John 4:11, we meet a woman who questioned Jesus when He offered to completely satisfy her needs as well. Like me, her desires were endless; the well of her soul was deep. But that day, as they talked, Jesus showed her *what* she was looking for and *where* she could find it, just like He had done with me—and just like He wants to do with you.

Proverbs 19:22 says, "What a [woman] desires is unfailing love." The word "desire" comes from the Hebrew word *ta'avah*, which means to greatly long for, to deeply desire or crave. Interestingly, unfailing love is mentioned thirty-two times in the Bible, and not once is it attributed to a person. It is only attributed to God.

God gave us a need for unfailing love because He knew it would lead us back to Him. All He needs is His Spirit who draws us to Him. And as far as the depth of the well goes, it is our heart He is looking into, and we're the only one who can stop Him from reaching the deep and hidden parts that need Him most.

Will you invite Jesus to look into the well of your heart today so He can show you what, who, and where you might be looking to be filled and fulfilled? Then ask Him to fill and fulfill you with the promise and reality of His unfailing love instead.

Jesus, help me stop searching for fulfillment in anything or anyone but You. Like King David, I pray You will satisfy me every morning with Your unfailing love, and that I will depend on You to meet my deepest desires and needs. In Your name, Amen.

When I say: I'll never be content.

God **says:** Let My unfailing love satisfy the longings of your heart.

What a [woman] desires is unfailing love. (Prov. 19:22)

26

When You Feel Like Damaged Goods

You will be a crown of splendor in the LORD's hand, a
royal diadem in the hand of your God.

Isaiah 62:3

She walked down the aisle of the discount grocery store looking for a bargain she couldn't resist. It was always hit and miss in this store . . . and she had missed . . . *again*.

But then Carol passed by a bin that caught her eye. It was labeled "Damaged Goods."

She told me it was filled with dented cans and those that were missing labels. No real rhyme or reason to it, just random items that were not considered shelf-worthy.

Carol knew just how they felt. She'd learned many lessons in the school of hard knocks, lessons that left bruises and dents, and then slapped on a label that threatened to define who she was. "Life often delivers the unexpected, and we feel as if we have been tossed into a bin, no longer worthy of a place on the shelf. Sometimes we believe the lie that we are second-class failures and all hope is gone," she shared with me.

Carol leaned over the bin and intentionally chose a dented can with no label and decided to buy it, because there just might be something worthwhile inside.

When she got home, she placed it on the counter and listened with anxious anticipation to the whirr of the can opener. And finally, when the metal lid was removed, she discovered peaches. That's when she let out a schoolgirl squeal. Carol loves peaches. It was such a treat to open that can and be greeted by one of her favorite fruits. The can was damaged, yet the contents were not just good but also oh-so-sweet.

Carol told me she was sure God must have smiled, because at that moment a beam of sunshine slipped through her kitchen window. And she knew there was a lesson He wanted her to learn.

You see, Carol has been damaged. God knows she isn't living the life that she dreamed about when she was a kid. However, the damage that Carol has suffered through her unexpected and unwanted divorce has made the contents of her heart so much sweeter, so much more compassionate, so much more in pursuit of Jesus.

Sometimes Carol feels looked down on and even judged by those who have seen her label missing and slapped on their own.

She's wanted to say, "Don't judge too quickly. My damage has not defined me . . . but it is refining me."

Today if you start feeling like you're at the bottom of life's bin, remember Jesus paid as high a price for those of us who are damaged as He did for those who are proudly displayed on the top shelf.

Jesus, life hasn't turned out like I thought it would. But I know You can still use me. Please forgive me for labeling myself and measuring my value based on my circumstances instead of the work You are doing in me. In Your name I pray, Amen.

When I say: I feel like damaged goods.

God **says:** You are royalty to Me.

> You will be a crown of splendor in the LORD's hand,
> a royal diadem in the hand of your God. (Isa. 62:3)

27

Who Told You That You Were . . . ?

And he said, "Who told you that you were naked?"

Genesis 3:11

---

*D*o you ever stop and ask yourself, *What's wrong with me?* One day I noticed how many times I said that to myself. When I lost my keys, when I was mean to my husband, when I didn't keep a commitment, when I was late for a meeting, when I yelled at my kids, when I forgot to do something important—the list went on.

But that day I realized that every time I asked *What's wrong with me?* I was actually telling myself that something *was* wrong with me. Then I would try to figure out my elusive fault so I could change it. But what I needed to change was the way I talked to myself.

God doesn't want us telling ourselves that we're defective. However, we have an enemy who loves to cast a shadow of self-doubt over us by playing into our self-defeating thoughts. He tries to get us to focus on all that is *wrong* with us (real or perceived), instead of anything that is *right* with us.

Scripture tells us that when Satan lies, he speaks his native language, for he is a liar and the father of lies (John 8:44). The word *lie* means a falsehood with the intent to deceive. Satan *intends* to deceive our hearts by getting us to take our eyes off of who we are in Christ and focus on our flaws—then spend our days figuring out how we can hide them.

One of his goals is to get us to believe lies that leave us feeling inadequate and unsure of ourselves. It's just what he did with Eve in the garden. In fact, I wonder if Eve might have thought, *What's wrong with me?* when she became aware of her inadequacy.

> Then the eyes of both [Adam and Eve] were opened, and they realized they were naked; so they sewed fig leaves together and made coverings for themselves.
>
> Then the man and his wife heard the sound of the Lord God as he was walking in the garden . . . and they hid from the Lord God. . . . But the Lord God called to the man, "Where are you?"
>
> He answered, "I heard you in the garden, and I was afraid because I was naked; so I hid." (Gen. 3:7–10)

In verse 11 God responds with a question, asking Adam who told them they were naked. In other words, "Who told you that something is wrong with you?" By asking this, God acknowledged there was someone casting shame on them—and it wasn't Him.

I believe He wanted them to be aware of their enemy, who was whispering lies into their hearts and causing them to move away from Him and from each other. God also wants us to be aware that we have an enemy who is constantly trying to convince us that we're inadequate and that something is wrong with us.

Sadly, we often go along with Satan's lies and live like they are true. Rarely do we stop to ask, *Who is saying these things? Who is causing me to doubt myself? Is it me? Is there something from my past that led me to believe this? Or is it the enemy of my soul disguising his voice as my own?*

But we can change that starting today. First, we need to realize Satan's schemes are the same for us as they were for Eve. Second, we need to determine we are not going to keep falling into his traps. Instead we can refute his lies and accusations with truth. When you feel defeated or defective, stand on the promise that "In all these things [you] are more than [a conqueror] through him who loved [you]" (Rom. 8:37).

Period. The end. There is nothing wrong with you—and don't let Satan convince you otherwise.

Lord, help me recognize the enemy's accusations and my own self-doubts. Please remind me of Your unconditional love and help me turn away from the lies so I can listen to and live in Your truth! In Jesus' name, Amen.

When I say: What's wrong with me?

God **says:** When you feel defeated or defective, stand on the promise that you are more than a conqueror because of My love for you!

In all these things we are more than conquerors through him who loved us. (Rom. 8:37)

28

If God Is for Me . . .

What, then, shall we say in response to these things? If
God is for us, who can be against us?

Romans 8:31

I can't do it all! I'm not cut out to be a wife, a mom, a
daughter, a speaker, a writer, and all the other things God
has called me to.

I had barely woken up, yet I already felt beat up by feelings of
inadequacy. My thoughts were against me, and my feelings were too.

About that time, my radio alarm came on and my thoughts were
interrupted by Twila Paris singing. With confident assurance, she
spoke truth to my soul, telling me it was not a time for fear, but a
time for faith and determination. She challenged me not to lose my
vision or be carried away by my emotions, but to hold on to all that
I had hidden in my heart, and all I believed to be true. Then she
reminded me of the most important truth of all: God is in control.[1]

As I heard her words, my thoughts aligned with God's truth and
my perspective changed. I went from feeling afraid to feeling determined, from feeling out of control to knowing God is in control.

Every day we have a choice—either to let doubt beat us up or to let God's truth build us up. In the same way a radio has AM and FM frequencies, our thoughts do too. They are either AM (against me) or FM (for me) thoughts.

Honestly, we are often our worst critics and have a lot of AM thoughts. And if our thoughts are against us, our feelings will be too.

So the next time you get those feelings of inadequacy, stop and identify what it is you are thinking that is making you feel that way. Then compare your thoughts to God's thoughts found in the Bible. Do they match? If not, find a promise in God's Word to replace the lie that has filled your heart with doubt and start thinking about that promise. Even say it out loud and pray the words, asking God to make them true for you in that moment.

For instance, when doubt comes *against you*, telling you that you're weak and all alone, focus on the truth that God is *for you!* You can be strong and courageous because the Lord your God is with you. He promises to never leave you nor forsake you (Deut. 31:6).

Turn that truth into a prayer that reflects just how much God is for you. For instance, you can say: "God, I am so thankful that You are for me. Because You are for me and with me, I can be strong and courageous in this situation because You promise that You will never leave me nor forsake me. I'm choosing to think Your Word that is for me instead of listening to the doubts that so easily come against me."

We have full access to God's power and His promises to live with a confident heart. But it won't just happen because it's possible. We have to take action.

Just like I tuned in to that station the night before (so I'd wake up hearing encouraging music), let's get intentional about tuning our thoughts in to God's thoughts toward us, today and every day.

Lord, help me remember today that You are with me to fight for me against my enemies of insecurity and feelings of inadequacy. In all these things, I am more than a conqueror through Him who loves me. In Jesus' name, Amen.

When I say: Everything and everyone is against me.

God **says:** I am for you!

> What, then, shall [you] say in response to these things? If God is for [you], who can be against [you]? (Rom. 8:31)

29

Living in the "Hear" and Now

My sheep listen to my voice; I know them, and they follow me.

John 10:27

I sat on the couch looking out the window, wondering what the future held. Some opportunities were on the horizon, and my excitement, mixed with the fear of getting overcommitted, ignited a rapid firing of thoughts: *What should I say yes or no to? What is God calling me to do? How will I figure out His plans and purpose for my schedule?*

Wondering and worrying wasn't getting me anywhere, so I decided to start praying. I wrote questions in a notebook: "Lord, what should I say yes to? Where do You want me to spend my time? Will You please show me Your plans for me this coming year?"

I wanted a sneak peek into God's calendar so I could adjust mine. Instead, I sensed Him telling me not to worry about tomorrow but to live each day in the *hear* and *now*.

I'd done pretty well when it came to listening to God in the big things. It was when God called me to small acts of obedience behind the scenes that I was most challenged. A few weeks after my conversation with God and my commitment to listen more closely for His voice, I noticed my husband's side of the closet was a mess. I thought about how JJ enjoys things being orderly, although it's not his natural inclination.

I remembered how frazzled he'd seemed the day before. Then I sensed God whispering to my heart, *One way you could really love JJ and bring peace to his world would be to organize his side of the closet.*

He's a grown man; he can organize his own side of the closet. I have two kids, two dogs, and myself to keep up with. Have you seen our garage and attic? I thought.

Did you hear Me? Are you going to obey Me now? God's Spirit nudged.

Just that week I had read Matthew 25, and I realized my attitude was like that of the servant who wasn't a good steward of what his master entrusted to him. Sometimes I saw my roles of wife, mother, and friend as "average" responsibilities. *Plenty of people have the same assignments,* I thought. Without realizing it, I let myself slip into being selfish, inconsiderate, or impatient here and there.

Yet God wanted my willingness in every area of my life—hearing and acting on His promptings in my heart throughout my days.

Why does Jesus call us to moment-by-moment listening and obedience? Because He loves us and wants us to trust Him, knowing His ways are better than our own.

Obedience means actively exchanging our will for His. God knows it is hard for us to hear His voice and follow His plans for our tomorrows when we are not willing to obey Him in our todays. But He promises that when we are faithful with the little things, He will "put us in charge of many things" and give us a deeper joy than we have ever known (Matt. 25:21).

God will be patient as we learn to trust Him in the big and little things in life. And it's in our relationship with Him that we will find the purpose, direction, and meaning we're looking for. When we live in the "hear and now," our calling and our calendar begin to reflect our love for Him, not our need for fulfillment or the desire to be important in anyone's eyes but His.

By the way, I reorganized my husband's side of the closet. I think I might have heard God chuckle as I felt the warmth of His smile. May He smile on you today as you commit to live in the "hear and now"—acting on what you *hear* and living it out *now*.

Dear Lord, I want to be faithful with the assignments You've given me. Help me to listen and live the way You want me to. Today I commit to live in the hear and now, listening for Your leading throughout my day. In Jesus' name, Amen.

When I say: I don't know what God wants me to do.

God **says:** Listen closely for My voice and follow the promptings of your heart that are consistent with My ways and My Word.

My sheep listen to my voice; I know them,
and they follow me. (John 10:27)

30

When Hurt Steals Your Hope

May the God of hope fill you with all joy and peace as you trust in him, so that you may overflow with hope by the power of the Holy Spirit.

Romans 15:13

---

*H*ow could this be happening? She had given up so much to be with him.

My friend Susan had left her very successful career and her lifelong friends in Louisiana, uprooted her three kids, and moved to North Carolina to get married and live in her new husband's hometown.

And now, six years later, she answered the phone on a Sunday afternoon and was shocked by the confession of a woman who called to tell Susan she'd been having an affair with her husband—for four years.

I held Susan as she sobbed. And I listened as she questioned everything about her husband. Every business trip, every late night at the office, everything she thought was true was now laced with deceit.

Her pain pierced my heart and something in my soul cracked that day. Every bit of hope I ever had that I would one day get married . . . it was gone. And I swore that I would never, ever trust a man.

Has pain from your yesterdays or disappointment in your today ever stolen your hope? When you have been wounded, the risk of getting hurt again seems more costly, and perhaps even more likely, doesn't it?

The things that hurt us are as varied as the lies we believe because of them:

- Like my friend who was sexually abused by a neighbor when she was eight years old. Shame convinced her she would always be dirty and worthless.
- Like my friend who was raped at knifepoint by a masked stranger the week of her college graduation. Fear held her for years in a personal prison, convincing her she'd never be free.
- Like my friend who was married and divorced multiple times. Condemnation convinced her she'd never be good enough for a man or for God.
- Like a woman I know whose mother called her names and criticized everything she did. Humiliation held her hostage, convincing her she'd always be useless.
- Like my friend who had an abortion when she was a teenager. Paralyzing grief and disgrace convinced her God could never use her in ministry.
- Like my friend whose son was in prison awaiting trial as a sex offender. False blame kept her up at night, convincing her she must have done something wrong as a mom.

The pain of our past makes it hard to believe God's promise of hope for our future. It's easy to lose confidence in Him, in other people, and especially in ourselves.

Yet hope comes when we allow Jesus to search our hearts and bring truth into our wounded places. Today's key verse reminds us that He wants us to "trust in Him, so that [we will] overflow with hope by the power of the Holy Spirit" (Rom. 15:13).

And the only way that can happen is if we let Jesus pour His healing power into our lives, allowing His love to flow into our pain and cleanse the wounds from our past.

I watched Susan's heart break into pieces in the following months, as her future and her marriage were shattered by the lies. But I also watched her come to know God and fully rely on His love for her, over time.

I learned to trust and hope again too. And I made a new vow—I promised myself and God that I would not allow the pain of my past to determine my future anymore.

We don't have to allow our hurts to steal our hope. Instead we can ask Jesus to help us trust Him more through them. As we do, let's lean on Him to redefine our future—not through the filter of our past, but through the power of His hope-resurrecting promises.

Lord, You are good and I want to trust that You have good plans for me. But sometimes, people and circumstances rob me of that truth and cast a shadow on Your goodness. Please restore my trust and hope in You. I'm leaning on all You are. In Jesus' name, Amen.

When I say: I don't want to hope so I won't be disappointed.

God **says:** Let me fill you with My hope as you trust in Me today.

May the God of hope fill you with all joy and peace
as you trust in him, so that you may overflow with
hope by the power of the Holy Spirit. (Rom. 15:13)

31

I Just Don't Have It in Me

I have been crucified with Christ and I no longer live,
but Christ lives in me. The life I now live in the body, I
live by faith in the Son of God, who loved me and gave
himself for me.

Galatians 2:20

I was completely blindsided. I'd been called into a meeting
at my church with another woman in leadership who had
been upset with me for months. But I was just finding out about it.

Someone told her I didn't agree with her leadership style. But
that wasn't what I'd said—months before—in a meeting with several
other leaders. I had been asked my opinion about a situation
and had shared my thoughts. It broke my heart that I was just
being asked about it now, many months later.

We both volunteered countless hours in ministry, pouring our
hearts and lives into women in our church. All the while, we were
on the same team and assumed we fully supported one another.
But now the trust we'd built for years was unraveling.

It was a mess. *I was a mess.*

I decided I was done. I just didn't have it in me. I wasn't strong enough or resilient enough. And I was exhausted from the hurt I felt and the hurt I had caused.

That afternoon I went home and cried. Told God I was ready to call it quits. Laying my head down on my desk, I said I couldn't do it anymore.

But then a truth that had been buried deep in my heart surfaced: "I have been crucified with Christ and I no longer live, but Christ lives in me. The life I now live in the body, I live by faith in the Son of God, who loved me and gave himself for me" (Gal. 2:20).

And in that moment, I knew if I was willing to die to myself and completely rely on *Christ in me* I could experience His resurrection power in this place of depletion—where I had nothing left to give.

There was no way *around* this crossroad: I could either walk away from God's calling on my life or I could allow Jesus to live *His* life through me. I could die to my desire to protect myself from getting hurt again and choose to tap into His power by relying on the strength of His Spirit.

I wasn't enough . . . wasn't strong enough, resilient enough, or humble enough, *but Christ in me was more than enough.*

You see, Jesus did not die on the cross just to get us out of hell and into heaven. He died on the cross to get Himself out of heaven and into us! That is resurrection life—and the very place where we get our *enough!*

If you have been crucified with Christ, *you no longer live,* but Christ lives in you. The life you now live in your body, you can choose to live by faith in the Son of God, who loved you and gave Himself for you.

I opted to rely on the Holy Spirit within me as my friend and I navigated this tough leadership situation. It wasn't easy, but it was good and it helped restore our friendship. The next time you and I find ourselves at a tough relational crossroads—choosing between walking away from God's calling on our lives or allowing

Jesus to live His life through us—let's allow Him to be *enough*! For indeed He is.

Dear Lord, You are mighty, and holy, and strong. And I thank You that Your sweet Holy Spirit is more than enough to help me die to myself and let YOU live through me. In Jesus' name, Amen.

When I say: I just don't have it in me.

God **says:** Let Me give My life to you and live My life through you.

> I have been crucified with Christ and I no longer live, but Christ lives in me. The life I now live in the body, I live by faith in the Son of God who loved me and gave himself for me. (Gal. 2:20)

32

When You Feel Empty

My people have committed two sins: They have forsaken
me, the spring of living water, and have dug their own
cisterns, broken cisterns that cannot hold water.

Jeremiah 2:13

———————

*O*ur hearts leak and will always end up empty when we find
our worth in anything but who we are in Christ. Our value
is not measured by what others think of us—but we surely live like
it is, don't we? It's almost as though we wake up every morning
with an empty jar and walk around holding it out to people or
things, hoping they will fill us.

We look to our relationships, our stuff, and our status to define
us. From the time we are kids, we look to our parents, friends,
teachers, bosses, boyfriends, ministry leaders, or whoever else is in
a position of importance to us. We long for their approval because
it makes us feel significant.

As we get older, we look for someone who will bestow on us a
sense of beauty and belonging, of being chosen and wanted. We

put them in a place of preeminence, hoping they will finally be the one who can satisfy our longing for lasting love.

When people don't work, we look to the many possessions the world tells us we need: newer cars, bigger houses, and trendy clothes. We get a new car and we're so happy—until someone dings it in the parking lot or we spill coffee on the new carpet.

So we head to the mall to get a new outfit, and we feel so good—then we walk into a meeting and somebody else is wearing it too. All of a sudden the outfit is old and we don't feel so special anymore. Maybe if we could just get a new house or some new furniture, then we'd be content, right?

But that's not all. We vie for positions and put our hope in recognition. We want to be noticed and acknowledged, whether it's a calling in ministry, a corner office at work, a title on our door, a promotion, or even an education. We work hard to get to higher places—and then wonder why they are never enough.

Our schedules are full, our minds are full, our stomachs are full, our closets are full, our lives are full. Yet we find ourselves with so many empty places.

Why? Because we, like the people God is talking about in today's key verse, "have forsaken [Him], the spring of living water, and have dug [our] own cisterns, broken cisterns that cannot hold water" (Jer. 2:13).

Our broken cisterns leak because the wells of our hearts were created to be filled by God alone.

The deepest thirst of our souls can only be quenched by Him. Although the people and things I've listed are gifts, so many times we look to the gifts instead of the Giver to fill us and fulfill us with lasting contentment and significance.

So what do we do when our hearts start tossing and turning with discontent and uncertainty? We need to stop and ask Jesus to help us see the worth we are placing in other things and the worth we are seeking in other people. One thing that has helped me is to write when-then statements. For example:

When I start to measure my value by how well I am doing as a _____ (mom, wife, woman, friend, etc.), *then* I will thank God for the gift of my roles and for the gift of His unconditional love that determines my worth.

When I feel insecure about my position at work, church, or somewhere else, *then* I will thank God for the high or low position I have on earth and for my position in Christ that secures my significance forever.

When I feel an aching emptiness that I'm tempted to fill with food, television, or anything other than God, *then* I will thank God for being the strength of my heart and my portion forever—and remember that He is the One who satisfies the hunger and thirst of my soul.

Lord, help me focus on You, the Giver, so I can depend on You for my identity and purpose. By focusing on who You are instead of the things I want, I want to remember how much I have and how valuable I am in You and to You. In Jesus' name, Amen.

When I say: I feel so empty.

God **says:** I created you with a longing in your heart that only I can fill.

Satisfy us in the morning with your unfailing love, that we may sing for joy and be glad all our days. (Ps. 90:14)

33

Dealing with Disappointments

Show me your ways, LORD, teach me your paths. Guide me in your truth and teach me, for you are God my Savior, and my hope is in you all day long.

Psalm 25:4–5

---

ave you ever spent months working on something, with big expectations and high hopes . . . and then in the blink of an eye it was crushed? This reality tore into my friend Tracie's heart like a jagged knife, ripping her dream of writing a book into tiny shreds.

Her disappointment was so crushing she had a hard time managing her emotions. She had worked tirelessly over long days, for weeks and weeks, pouring all she had into her dream. Now all she had was disappointment and rejection.

Tracie shared how her disappointment became irritation, which morphed into resentment. She didn't *feel* like it was fair.

Why didn't God answer my prayers? Why had He placed a dream in my heart only to allow it to crumble? Why had He let this happen? Why me?

I knew I needed to have a good attitude and not give up, but I did not FEEL like doing that—at all!

Questions pummeled my thoughts: *What is the use? Why try again? If God didn't answer my prayer after all this time, why bother to keep trying?*

I allowed my feelings to overtake my faith.

All I could think about was how this disappointment made me *feel*, instead of what God may be doing that my faith could not see. I felt forgotten and like God's ways weren't fair, without remembering God's ways are best. I felt a longing for immediate results, instead of trusting that God's timing is perfect.

One afternoon I turned to Psalm 25, and these verses helped me find my way back to the assurance and perspective I needed:

Verse 1, *"In you, LORD my God, I put my trust."*

I felt discouraged, unworthy, hopeless, rejected. So I poured my feelings and my soul out to God. And He listened.

Verse 2, *"I trust in you; do not let me be put to shame, nor let my enemies triumph over me."*

God reminded me to trust Him, not a desire or a dream. Not the world's view. Not my abilities. Not my time frame. Not my ideas. Trust Him alone. I prayed about my enemies—intangible feelings such as self-doubt, insecurity, frustration, and discouragement.

Verse 3, *"No one who hopes in you will ever be put to shame, but shame will come on those who are treacherous without cause."*

Regardless of whether or not my desires become a reality, I will not be put to shame, because God is my God. If His plans coincide with my dreams, I know He will keep His promises and nothing can stop His purposes for my life.

Verses 4–5a, *"Show me your ways, LORD, teach me your paths. Guide me in your truth and teach me."*

These words stopped me in my tracks. I began to think more rationally. Why had I been beating my head against a wall? Why was I consumed with anxiety and frustration? Was I allowing God to direct my paths? God gently reminded me He is the teacher, I am the student.

Verse 5b, "*For you are God my Savior, and my hope is in you all day long.*"[1]

Tracie learned that if she put her hope in her own desires and abilities, she would set herself up for disappointment. And that is so true for each of us. Our only hope for joy and fulfillment comes from banking our joy and confidence in Christ alone. Hope is found in Him, not people, a career, a husband or children, church, financial success, or dreams that come true.

Disappointments will happen. With God, however, we can turn those disappointments into God's appointments to trust Him.

Dear Lord, You know the hurt in my heart and the sting of disappointments I have experienced. Please help me trust You, instead of being consumed by my wounded emotions. Empower me with faith that is stronger than my feelings. In Jesus' name, Amen.

When I say: I'm so disappointed.

God **says:** Let Me show you My ways in this disappointment and guide your emotions with My truth.

Show me your ways, LORD, teach me your paths. Guide me in your truth and teach me, for you are God my Savior, and my hope is in you all day long. (Ps. 25:4–5)

34

Measuring Up

*When they measure themselves by themselves and compare
themselves with themselves, they are not wise.*

2 Corinthians 10:12

———————

o you ever feel like you don't quite measure up? Maybe
you think you're not as smart, capable, personable, or
godly as a lot of the people you know.

It is so easy to think that if we had more or knew more, we'd be
secure. But the truth is, even people who "have it all" still struggle
with feelings of insecurity. The Bible opens with the story of a
woman who had everything, but it wasn't enough (Gen. 2).

God had established Eve's worth as His child and the crown
of His creation. He also gave Eve every woman's desire: intimacy,
beauty, security, significance, and purpose. Yet Satan conjured up
feelings of insecurity by getting Eve to take her eyes off what she
had and focus on what she didn't have.

Boy, can I relate. Like Eve, I've heard Satan's whispers telling me
I'm not all I could be—or should be. One day I was reading her
story in Genesis 2 and I noticed that his questions and suggestions

were intended to plant seeds of doubt in Eve's heart. He wanted her to doubt God and herself.

The enemy's whispers tempted Eve to try to "be" more and "have" more by seeking significance apart from God's provision. He convinced her something was missing in her life and that the forbidden fruit would make her be "like God."

It was a foolish comparison, but all comparisons are. Yet don't we do it all the time? *If only I was like her . . . if only I had a house like hers, a husband like hers, a job like hers . . . if only my children behaved like hers . . . If only _____, then I'd feel significant, satisfied, and secure.*

In today's key verse, Paul warns us that those who "measure themselves by themselves, and compare themselves with themselves, are not wise" (2 Cor. 10:12). Comparison will always leave us feeling like we don't measure up. We can try to do more and be more, yet it's never enough.

If only Eve had focused on who she was and what she had as a child of God. If only we could too.

Yet Satan wants us to focus on our flaws and feelings of inadequacy, then exhaust our energy figuring out how to hide them. But we don't have to go along with his schemes. Instead we can recognize his lies, refute his temptations with truth, and focus on God's acceptance, security, and significance. Then we can thank God for His provision and His promises that remind us of who we are in Him.

I am accepted

Ephesians 1:3–8	I have been chosen by God and adopted as His child.
Colossians 1:13–14	I have been redeemed and forgiven of all my sins.
Colossians 2:9–10	I am complete in Christ.

I am secure

Romans 8:28	I am assured that God works for my good in all circumstances.
Romans 8:31–39	I am free from condemnation. I can't be separated from God's love.

| Philippians 1:6 | I am confident God will complete the good work He started in me. |

I am significant

Ephesians 2:10	I am God's workmanship.
Ephesians 3:12	I may approach God with freedom and confidence.
Philippians 4:13	I can do all things through Christ, who strengthens me.

Dr. Neil T. Anderson says, "The more you reaffirm who you are in Christ, the more your behavior will begin to reflect your true identity."[1] So, when you're tempted to use the measuring stick of comparison, be sure to measure UP by focusing upward on Christ—remembering whose you are and who you are *in* HIM!

Lord, thank You that in Christ I'm accepted, secure, and significant. When I'm tempted to find my significance and security apart from Your provision and promises, help me recognize Satan's lies, refuse his temptations, and stand firm in my faith. In Jesus' name, Amen.

When I say: I'll never measure up.

God **says:** Don't use the measuring stick of comparison. Instead, measure up by focusing upward on Christ—remembering who you are in Him.

He who began a good work in you will carry it on to completion until the day of Christ Jesus. (Phil. 1:6)

35

You Are Good Enough

*"For your Maker is your husband—the LORD Almighty
is his name—the Holy One of Israel is your Redeemer;
he is called the God of all the earth. The LORD will call
you back as if you were a wife deserted and distressed in
spirit—a wife who married young, only to be rejected,"
says your God.*

Isaiah 54:5–6

---

*M*ike and I had what felt like a storybook Christian
romance. He was tall, dark, and handsome. He had a
successful business and he loved Jesus. But to top it all off, instead
of asking me out for a date, he asked if we could "court."

We got along great and everyone said we'd make the perfect
couple in life and in ministry. Eventually we started praying about
marriage and talked to our pastor about our future together. Not
too long after, Mike proposed.

But two weeks into our engagement he sat across a table, looked
into my eyes, and said, "I've made a horrible mistake. You are not
the one God wants me to marry."

I was devastated and wondered what I'd done to make God change His mind.

It took almost a year, but I eventually recovered and decided it would be safe to let guys within twenty feet of me again. Soon after, Mike showed up in my life, and asked me to consider building our friendship back again.

I was hesitant, yet I wondered if God wanted to redeem our story, so I gave him a second chance. We spent time with friends and took things slowly. But eventually we talked about marriage again. He proposed again. I accepted again. And he dumped me again!

That time I got smart and didn't give the ring back. Instead I held it as collateral to get Mike to go to a counselor. It didn't take long for the counselor to let us know Mike had a fear of commitment. Having a name for it made me feel a little better, but Mike felt horrible and ashamed.

One night I felt a deep sense of concern for him, so I drove to his apartment. When I got there, I felt compelled to get in his van and pray for him. Afterward I opened my eyes and noticed his journal sitting on the console.

Turning to the entries he'd written when he'd called off our engagement, I came face-to-face with why he thought I wasn't good enough. There were things about my personality and my body size he wished were different. His words opened a deep wound. You see, I grew up with a father, a stepfather, and brothers who looked at pornography. From the time I was a little girl, I feared I would have to be perfect to be loved and I knew I never would be.

After I read Mike's journal, every time I stood in front of a mirror, doubt whispered: *No man will ever want you. You'll never be good enough.*

Rejection. Betrayal. Abandonment. Our greatest fears can become the reality of our worst nightmare. Maybe your father abandoned you, or your husband cheated on you. Maybe your best friend broke your trust, or your teenager has shut you out.

The deep pain we feel as a result of broken relationships can make us doubt we are valuable. We begin to see ourselves as disposable. Easily replaced. Not good enough.

One day my pastor told me something I'll never forget. He said, "Renee, you can't put your hope in a man, you can only put your hope in God. A man's love will always disappoint you."

I had always put my hope in finding a man to love me. Now I had to separate myself, and my worth, from a man's decision to want me or not. I had to hold Mike's words and his preferences up to God's Word.

One morning I read Isaiah 54:5–6, and God showed me He is my Maker and my Husband, my Redeemer—the One who bestows the honor and acceptance I long for.

The promise that He chose me as His own was the only assurance I could hold on to. Once God's unfailing love was all I had, I realized His unfailing love was all I needed.

Although people's preferences will change, God's desire for us won't. Others might not think we're good enough, but God always will. And even if someone decides they don't desire us anymore, God most certainly does! The truth is, when we belong to Jesus we are loved and accepted forever.

We are covered in His goodness, and it's His goodness that makes us good enough!

Jesus, I want to know and rely on the love You have for me, and live in that love. You say that whoever lives in love lives in You, and You in him. In this way, love is made complete in me, so that I can have confidence today and forever. In Your name, Amen.

When I say: I'm not good enough.

God **says:** You are covered in My goodness, and My goodness makes you good enough!

> For your Maker is your husband—the LORD
> Almighty is his name—the Holy One of
> Israel is your Redeemer. (Isa. 54:5)

36

Before the Battle Begins

Finally, be strong in the Lord and in his mighty power. . . .
Take the helmet of salvation and the sword of the Spirit,
which is the word of God. And pray in the Spirit on all
occasions with all kinds of prayers and requests.

Ephesians 6:10, 17–18

For years, Julie walked around with a destructive mind-set and didn't even recognize it. Raised in a tumultuous home that simmered with anger, resentment, and critical words, she picked up deadly thought processes early on. Sadly, Julie considered it completely normal.

Critical thoughts spread like weeds throughout her mind and threatened to choke out every positive thought. Years later, Julie found herself enduring a miserable marriage and regularly crying herself to sleep.

I was still unaware that negative mindsets poisoned my thoughts. Thinking the best of others was foreign to me. Each morning I'd wake up and rehash my husband's harsh words of the night before.

I'd tell myself things were never going to change, and meditate on my critical thoughts and feelings. I was extremely unhappy.

My unhealthy mindset made it hard to forgive, because I replayed hurtful words and situations in my mind over and over. It's very difficult (if not impossible!) to forgive what you regularly focus on. This set up a destructive cycle in my marriage. Instead of forgiving and letting go, I rehearsed the hurt and held on. And I always thought it was warranted because I felt my husband's words and actions toward me were wrong.[1]

One weekend Julie went away on a women's retreat, and during a time of reflective prayer, God helped her to see how her constant stream of critical thoughts toward her husband was destroying their relationship.

That is when she started to understand that even though her husband's actions toward her might be wrong, her response as a Christian was just as wrong. Change was slow but steady as Julie submitted to God's leading.

Over time my mindset slowly changed, but it remained a real effort not to give in to the negative thoughts I had regularly entertained most of my life. It took time and concerted effort, but as I prayed God's Word and spent time reading my Bible, wrong mindsets were replaced with healthy, godly thoughts.[2]

Whether we battle a negative or critical attitude, bitterness, insecurity, worry, or fearful thoughts, we must recognize the enemy's battle plan to consistently assault our minds until we surrender.

Usually, his attacks are subtle. Often they seem like our own thoughts. Most of the time we simply agree with Satan's whispers of condemnation and critical thoughts toward ourselves and others without even recognizing what we are doing.

We have a choice: let the enemy win or let God's battle plan kick in.

In Ephesians 6:17–18, God gives us instructions for protecting the battlefield of our minds: "Take the helmet of salvation and the sword of the Spirit, which is the word of God. And pray in the Spirit on all occasions with all kinds of prayers and requests. With this in mind, be alert and always keep on praying."

We can resist the enemy and win the battle through God's Word and prayer. Combining the two is the most powerful weapon. Also, Romans 10:17 tells us, "faith *comes* from hearing, and hearing by the word of Christ" (NASB), so let's pray God's promises out loud.

When we pray God's words out loud, and hear them, the Holy Spirit engraves them on our hearts and writes them in our thoughts. As we internalize God's truth by internalizing His promises, we determine our victory before the battle even begins.

Jesus, help me rely on the power of Your Word to win the battle in my mind. I am putting on the full armor You offer me and taking up the sword of Your Spirit through prayer! In Your powerful name, Amen.

When I say: I feel so weak.

God **says:** Don't let Satan wear you down. Protect your mind with truth, and pray in the power of My promises every day.

Finally, be strong in the Lord and in his mighty power. . . . Take the helmet of salvation and the sword of the Spirit, which is the word of God. And pray in the Spirit on all occasions with all kinds of prayers and requests. (Eph. 6:10, 17–18)

37

A New Pattern of Thought

Do not conform to the pattern of this world, but be transformed by the renewing of your mind.

Romans 12:2

---

*I*t's usually very subtle. Sometimes I'll think about something I want to do or sense God calling me to, and a feeling of uncertainty comes over me. Doubt whispers to my heart, *You can't do that. You're not good enough.* Out of the blue, I'll get that awful, insecure feeling.

Too many times in the past I've gone along with my doubts. And without realizing what I was doing, I agreed with insecurities and aligned my heart with a sense of uncertainty.

For years, though, I didn't tell anyone about my doubts. I figured if they knew all the reasons I doubted myself, they'd notice flaws I had worked hard to hide. And honestly, I thought I was the only one who struggled with doubt.

However, I didn't call it doubt. Maybe you don't either. Sometimes I called it worry—worry that I was going to disappoint someone, worry that I might make a mistake and get criticized for it, worry that I might start something but not be able to finish.

Other times I called it fear—fear of not measuring up, fear of rejection, fear of looking prideful by thinking I could do something special for God.

What I've realized over the past several years is that these feelings may end up as fear or worry, but their source is self-doubt. Looking back, I see there was a pattern in my thinking that led to the pattern of my doubting.

As a child I thought I wasn't worth keeping. My insecurity kept me from riding the carousel at an amusement park, because I doubted my dad would wait for me. In school, I thought I wasn't smart enough. I avoided some great opportunities because they came with the risk of failure.

Even as a young bride, I doubted my worth in my husband's eyes. Although he gave me no reason to fear, our newlywed memories include a lot of arguments about trust.

The apostle Paul challenges us in Romans 12:2 to not let our minds be conformed to the patterns of this world. This means I need to take my patterns of thought into consideration because they affect what I believe about myself and what I believe about God's view of me and others.

The world's patterns of thought tell us our worth is measured by our weight or our bank account, our job or our spouse, by the number of friends we have or if we are able to have children. And if we do have children, the world tells us we're only good parents if our children behave "just so."

Have any of these thoughts ever held you back or convinced you that you don't have what it takes to be all God's calling you to be?

I think it happens to us more than we realize. Just this week, doubt tried to convince me I couldn't handle my life. I had a sick teenager, a book deadline, speech and occupational therapy appointments for my daughter, and very concerning health problems with my mom.

Remembering the wisdom in today's key verse, I paused to consider the pattern of my thoughts, and I knew they didn't line up with God's thoughts. For instance, in Philippians 4:13 God tells me, "I can do everything through Christ, who gives me strength" (NLT).

I started claiming that promise by weaving it into my thoughts, knowing I *could* do it all if I depended on the strength God promised to give me. And when I did, God transformed my heart by renewing my mind with His peace and perspective.

It takes time to replace our thoughts with God's thoughts. The ways of the world—fear and worry—are powerful forces. But God's Word trumps them, always. Today, let's be intentional in laying down our self-doubts and replacing them with truth instead, remembering that "He who began a good work in you will perfect it until the day of Christ Jesus" (Phil. 1:6 NASB).

Lord, I want to become a woman with a confident heart in Christ. I want to persevere in Your truth so that when I have done Your will, I will receive what You have promised. I am free from fear and worry. When doubt or insecurity tells me I can't do something, I will remember that all things are possible to her who believes. In Jesus' name, Amen.

When I say: I can't stop thinking negative thoughts.

God **says:** Let Me renew your mind and transform your thinking with My thoughts toward you.

Do not conform to the pattern of this world, but be
transformed by the renewing of your mind. (Rom. 12:2)

38

No More Guilt-Induced Doubt

Let us then approach God's throne of grace with confi-
dence, so that we may receive mercy and find grace to help
us in our time of need.

Hebrews 4:16

---

everal years ago I blew it and felt sure God was ready to
give up on me.

I was at my mom's house writing message outlines for our
church's women's retreat where I'd be speaking in a month. My
mom offered her home one Saturday so I could spend time alone
preparing while she was running errands.

She said she would be gone all day until JJ came to pick me up
at 5:30 for a surprise party we were attending that night. Studying
in Mom's quiet house helped me get into a great writing "zone."
It was the perfect setting . . . until she came home—early.

She was quiet, for about thirty seconds. Then she brought ce-
ment pavers in and dropped them on the floor, and plopped down
groceries in the kitchen where I was studying.

Panic set in. I didn't have my message outlines complete and obviously my time was up. And as I put my notes away, I knocked a water bottle over onto my laptop. Mopping up the mess, I felt my chest tighten with anxiety and my eyes sting with tears. Before I knew it, I was running late getting ready.

At 5:40, I realized JJ wasn't there and I didn't want to ruin the surprise party by being late, so I decided he could meet me there.

As I pulled out of the driveway, JJ drove up. And much to my surprise he didn't hurry out of his car. In fact, my then-six-year-old son got out of the car, walked up to me, and said, "Daddy told us you would be mad." And I was!

As I passed JJ's car, he waved for me to stop and asked, "Aren't you going to wait for me?" Being all calm and mature, I said, "No. Because you're acting like an [beep]." (You know, the biblical word for mule.)

My eight-year-old son walked out right then and heard me. "Mommy! You just called Daddy an [beep]!" he exclaimed.

My mom heard the whole thing too, and added her sentiments: "And you call yourself a Christian speaker?"

I was overwhelmed with shame and guilt. How could I go from such a sweet place spiritually to such an ugly place emotionally? Shame set in. I had no business teaching a message I couldn't even live.

I'm not cut out for this. I'm not godly enough. What was God thinking when He called me to this? The next morning I found my women's ministry director and mentor, Mary Ann, at church. After I confessed what happened, I told her I needed to step down from being the retreat speaker.

She responded, "Renee, if you don't need this message as much as the women attending, then you are not qualified to teach it. But because you need it as much as we do, you are qualified. You have been appointed and you are anointed to do this."

I had never experienced such a demonstration of God's grace.

Does guilt-induced doubt ever deplete your confidence? It's hard to believe God could use us when we're such a mess, yet we don't have to look far to find men and women in Scripture whom He used greatly—despite their downfalls.

Mary Ann's response showed me what it looks like to "approach God's throne of grace with confidence, so that we may receive mercy and find grace to help us in our time of need" (Heb. 4:16).

Although we give up on ourselves, God doesn't. Instead, He can take what feels like destruction and use it for reconstruction in our grace-walk with Him.

When we confess our sins and receive God's forgiveness, our hearts are set free from guilt-induced doubt, and He offers to replace it with grace-infused confidence (1 John 1:9).

I spoke at the retreat and knew God wanted me to share what happened. Although I feared women might judge me, instead they loved knowing I wasn't perfect. Aren't you glad you don't have to be either?

Lord, I come to You today to receive mercy and find grace to help me. Will You replace my guilt-induced doubt with grace-infused confidence? In Jesus' name, Amen.

When I say: I've blown it and I feel so guilty!

God **says:** Give Me the guilt, and I will replace it with mercy and grace to help in your time of need.

Let us then approach God's throne of grace with
confidence, so that we may receive mercy and find
grace to help us in our time of need. (Heb. 4:16)

39

He Cares about You

Give all your worries and cares to God, for he cares about
you.

1 Peter 5:7 NLT

When life gets overwhelming, do you ever wonder if God notices everything you have going on—like how you're trying so hard to take care of everyone and everything? Staying up late to pay the bills and feeling stretched between relationships at home and in ministry—while caring for aging parents, commuting to work, and carpooling kids?

Several years ago, I couldn't keep up with all of the commitments I'd made. I felt like I was suffocating under everything I needed to do. Slowly, I let worry weave its way into my thoughts, making me wonder how I was going to do it all. I knew I should trust God more, but I was concerned that if I stopped worrying about everything and everybody, He would too.

Eventually, I came to a point where I was exhausted and ready to resign from just about everything. I ran out of fuel. I didn't have enough energy to handle all of my roles, relationships, and responsibilities.

I also ran out of faith. I started doubting my ability to manage my life, to hear God clearly, and to do all I assumed He wanted me to do.

And all those worries that made me weary also made me wonder. I wondered why God wasn't doing something to make my life easier. I wondered if God noticed and cared about all I was doing for Him and for others.

One day I was reading my Bible and noticed how Martha's worries were making her wonder if Jesus cared that her sister left her in the kitchen to do all that work by herself. "She came to him and asked, 'Lord, don't you care that my sister has left me to do the work by myself? Tell her to help me!'" (Luke 10:40).

Listen to how He responded: "'Martha, Martha,' the Lord answered, 'you are worried and upset about many things, but only one thing is needed. Mary has chosen what is better and it will not be taken away from her'" (vv. 41–42).

In that moment, Jesus showed Martha just how much He cared. Instead of giving her what she demanded, He showed Martha what she needed. Although she wanted help so she could get things done, Jesus knew Martha's need for control and perfection was making her come undone!

Jesus helped her see the distractions and preparations that had pulled her away from Him, and that He wanted her to spend time with Him more than He wanted her to serve Him.

Jesus also showed Martha that Mary hadn't left her to do all the work by herself. She had chosen what was better—what couldn't be taken away from her. It was one thing that would last even after He was gone: time with Him spent resting in His presence, soaking in His perspective, and listening to His promises. First Peter 5:7 tells us to "Give all your worries and cares to God, for he cares about you" (NLT).

As I read this verse and Martha's story, I saw the difference in what God wanted and what Martha and I had been doing. Jesus invites us to come to Him and cast our cares upon Him, so that *He can* care for us. When we do all the talking and instructing, He doesn't have a chance.

Instead of telling God what I needed, I learned how to say, "Lord, this is what's on my mind. This is what I'm worried about," and then ask, "Lord, what is going on in my heart? What are Your thoughts about this situation? What do I need to do?"

Jesus, help me learn how to seek You as much as I serve You and others. I want to balance my life and give my workload to You, knowing with confidence that You care about me and are good at taking care of me! In Jesus' name, Amen.

When I say: No one cares about all that is concerning me.

God **says:** Give your cares to Me, and let Me care for you.

Give all your worries and cares to God, for
he cares about you. (1 Pet. 5:7 NLT)

40

Dare to Hope

Yet I still dare to hope when I remember this.

Lamentations 3:21 NLT

---

*G*od *works all things together for good. God has a plan for your life.* What do these promises evoke in your heart? Do you believe they are true, or do you sometimes doubt them?
I've doubted and believed. It's easy to believe God's promises when life is going well. Yet few of us have walked this far without experiencing brokenness along the way. Many of us have had the wind completely knocked out of us, and wondered if we would ever have the strength to hope again.

My friend Wendy remembers long nights of crying herself to sleep, nights when she felt like everything she'd hoped for from the Lord was lost:

> Some nights, only silent tears trickled; other nights, loud wails accompanied questions and prayers. "Why, Lord? What am I doing wrong? Why won't You fix this?" My prayers ended with, "If it is Your will," hoping His will was different than it appeared to be.

Many nights I curled up in a ball under my covers, hoping for a breakthrough. Yet the situation seemed hopeless; I believed everything I had hoped for was lost.

Jeremiah, also known as the weeping prophet in the Old Testament, found himself in a hopeless situation too. He watched the temple of the Lord being burned to the ground by the Babylonians. Jeremiah's heart broke as the elements of the temple, such as the water basin and lamp snuffers, were stolen and taken to Babylon to be used to worship false gods.

In the midst of the devastation, Jeremiah prophesied God's words to the people of Judah and Jerusalem. Unfortunately, it wasn't good news. The Lord's immediate future for His people was one of discipline and the utter destruction of Jerusalem as well as His holy temple. Jeremiah was chosen by God to deliver these words to His people. Jeremiah did his job and did it well, but not without punishment, ridicule, insults, and imprisonment by the recipients of the news.

Jeremiah shed tears until he said, "I have cried until the tears no longer come; my heart is broken" (Lam. 2:11 NLT). His heart was broken for Jerusalem and for God's people, his people. In anguish Jeremiah lamented, "Everything I had hoped for from the Lord is lost" (3:18 NLT).

Then, in the midst of his despair, he dared. He dared to hope in what he remembered.

Many of us need hope. To find it like Jeremiah did, let's look at what he remembered that gave him the courage to dare to hope again. What Jeremiah remembered was the key to elevating him from the pit of despair to a place of expectancy. It is our key as well. Jeremiah remembered this about the Lord:

- His unfailing love
- His new mercies
- His never-ending faithfulness
- His inheritance

God's Word is just as alive and active today as it was in Jeremiah's day. It is designed to transform us from the inside-out. Reading and applying its truths will redirect our perspective.

During my desperate nights I longed for my circumstances to be different. I cried until the tears would no longer come. Many times I tarried in the pit of despair much longer than necessary. But when I remembered God's faithfulness and mercies to me, my hope was renewed.[1]

Wendy's circumstances didn't change the night she remembered God's promises. But what did change? Hope slipped into her outlook.

Do you need hope today? Do you need to remember God's unfailing love, His new mercies, His never-ending faithfulness, His inheritance promised to you—despite your heartache or fear of being disappointed if things don't turn out the way you want them to? Let's take the courageous step our heart needs and dare to hope again.

Dear Lord, I want to be brave. Help me dare to hope by remembering Your faithfulness, love, and mercy. Thank You for giving me the courage to have hope and the wisdom to choose not to put my hope in what I am hoping for! In Jesus' name, Amen.

When I say: I have lost all hope.

God **says:** Put your hope in Me. My love never ends and My compassion never fails.

> Yet I still dare to hope when I remember this: The faithful love of the LORD never ends! His mercies never cease. Great is his faithfulness. (Lam. 3:21–23 NLT)

41

You've Got Something
Special to Offer

*For if the willingness is there, the gift is acceptable ac-
cording to what one has, not according to what one does
not have.*

2 Corinthians 8:12

I opened my front door and saw my friend Janet standing
there. Before I could invite her in she said, "Renee, this
is the best thank-you note I've ever read. You have a writing gift
and you need to use it."

I was confused; it was *only* a thank-you note. Yet Janet's words
of affirmation stayed with me all afternoon.

My journal was filled with pages of me asking God for direction
in how I might serve in our new church. Doubt had convinced me
I had nothing special to offer.

Was this God's answer? Did He want me to encourage more
than just one friend with my writing?

Later that month I attended a dinner series at our church and took notes on a napkin. On the way home I wished we had been given a message outline. Then I got the craziest idea: *Maybe I could write a study guide to give to other women who want to go deeper too.*

Quickly, insecurity filtered my idea through reality. *Who am I to think I could write something other women would want to read?*

When I couldn't get the idea out of my head, I eventually told Janet about it. Much to my shock she told me the women's ministry team had been praying for a gift to give the women after the dinners.

A few weeks later, they asked me to write a study guide. I nearly suffocated under the weight of insecurity, but with Janet's prayers and prodding I wrote it, and over a thousand copies were given away. Then I wrote another the next year, and then another.

Honestly, I never really felt like I had anything special to offer, but I deeply sensed God wanted me to offer what I had, reminding me, "if the willingness is there, the gift is acceptable according to what one has, not according to what one does not have" (2 Cor. 8:12).

God loves when our hearts are willing to trust Him. And He loves to entrust us with more when we're good stewards of the special abilities He's given us.

Yet many times we let self-doubt shape our excuses, insisting: "I don't have any talent. I can't sing. I can't lead. I don't have anything special to offer."

No matter how big or small our abilities seem, they are all God-given and can be used for His purposes. I never thought I could write a book. I didn't even think I could write an article. But I loved writing thank-you notes, and that is what God used to show me how to use my ability to help others.

Whatever your natural talents are, when you make yourself available to share your divine abilities God works through you to meet the needs of other individuals and the church as a whole.

Lord, what abilities have You given me that I don't see? Make me aware of little things that can make a difference for You and others. I lay down my doubt, my envy, and my comparisons. I want to know the joy of being faithful with what You've given me. In Jesus' name, Amen.

When I say: I have nothing special to offer.

God **says:** I have entrusted you with gifts and abilities to serve Me and others.

> For if the willingness is there, the gift is acceptable according to what one has, not according to what one does not have. (2 Cor. 8:12)

42

When You Feel Far from God

*For it is by grace you have been saved, through faith—and
this is not from yourselves, it is the gift of God—not by
works, so that no one can boast.*

Ephesians 2:8–9

I used to feel far from God, like I had to work my way back
to Him whenever I did something wrong. It would happen after I did things that I considered to be "bad behavior" for
a Christian girl like me. Sometimes it happened after a conflict I
didn't handle so well, or after I promised to spend time with God
every day but didn't keep my promise long.

Other times I would feel distant from God after a hardship
that made me question His love or His presence in my life. Those
awful feelings of condemnation and distance would convince me
God was upset with my unbelief, and I needed to prove my faith
to Him again.

I would try harder to please Him or believe in Him, but no matter how hard I tried, eventually I would end up back in the same

place of wondering if this time I couldn't work my way back into God's favor.

And then one day I read about grace: God's *undeserved* favor.

That word *undeserved* told me I didn't have to behave right to earn God's love or favor, or work my way back when I felt far from Him. It meant that no matter how consistent or inconsistent, how good or bad, how believing or unbelieving I was, God wouldn't take away His favor.

The more I read about God's grace, the more determined I became to live in the freedom of His favor. And when those feelings of distance came, I learned to discern if they were feelings of godly conviction or Satan's tactics of condemnation.

Over time, I realized one of the reasons I doubted God's love is because we have an enemy "who uses every little offense to accuse us of being good-for-nothings," says Dr. Neil T. Anderson. "But your advocate Jesus Christ is more powerful than your adversary. He has cancelled the debt of your sins past, present, and future. No matter what you do or how you fail, God has no reason not to love you and accept you completely."[1]

The truth is, God's Spirit will convict us, but His heart will never condemn us.

So how do we know if we are hearing the voice of condemnation that comes from our accuser, or the voice of conviction that comes from God? Condemnation sweeps across our thoughts with generalized statements such as, *You're such a failure*, *You're so hypocritical*, or *You can never be counted on*. That is the accuser. His tone is condemning, questioning, and confusing. His accusations lead to guilt and shame.

In contrast, the Holy Spirit's conviction will be specific. He will reveal a sinful action or attitude and instruct us on what we need to do to right the wrong, whether it's restoring a broken relationship or returning something that isn't ours. He'll give us steps we need to take to change our behavior or attitude.

- Instead of *You're such a failure*, the Spirit might say, *You were really critical the way you talked to _____. You need to ask for forgiveness. Then tell them something that will build them up instead of tearing them down.*
- Instead of *You can never be counted on*, the Spirit might say, *You didn't keep your promise to _____ today. Call her to apologize and set up a lunch date for this weekend.*

God lovingly uses conviction to show us our sin and lead our hearts to repentance. He does this to draw us away from destructive behavior that hinders our relationship with Him and with others.

His desire is to bring us out of the darkness of our selfishness or self-sufficiency by leading us back into the light of His love, so we can walk in the freedom of forgiveness and the favor of His grace.

Dear Jesus, thank You for Your undeserved favor. I'm so grateful You never condemn me but that You do convict me. It's Your kindness that leads me to repentance and back into a place of restoration with You and with others. Help me remember and receive the lavish grace You offer when my heart feels far from You. In Your name, Amen.

When I say: I feel far from God, and like I need to work my way back to Him.

God **says:** I am here offering grace and truth to remind you there is no condemnation for those who are in Christ Jesus.

For it is by grace you have been saved, through faith—and this is not from yourselves, it is the gift of God—not by works, so that no one can boast. (Eph. 2:8–9)

43

Freedom from the Grave

*Then they cried to the LORD in their trouble, and he saved
them from their distress. He sent out his word and healed
them; he rescued them from the grave.*

Psalm 107:19–20

---

*A*s she sat in her psychology class, Stephanie's face turned
red and her heart raced. A few days earlier, a cardiolo-
gist had given her a monitor, instructing her to hit a button on it
every time her heart sped up. It was happening again, and this
time in a classroom.

That day, her class just happened to be learning about people
who have frequent physical complaints with no organic cause.
She couldn't help but wonder if that would be her diagnosis. In
her words:

*What if my heart issues were nothing more than stress and anxi-
ety? I actually hoped the doctor would find something physically
wrong with my heart so she wouldn't scrawl "crazy girl" on my
medical chart.*

Over the next few months, with more testing, Stephanie's doctor determined low thyroid levels were the organic basis for her heart problems. She started taking prescription medication; however, her heart issues continued. Curious as to why, she began to write down what was happening each time her heart raced.

Her list included the time she made a class presentation and when she walked alone in a dark parking lot. It happened when Stephanie faced confrontation and when certain people came around her. After a week of writing these triggers down, she recognized her heart issues were partly related to anxiety.

"A Christian girl shouldn't struggle with anxiety, should she?" Stephanie questioned. She shared with me,

> I wanted desperately to hide the struggle attacking me physically and emotionally, but it was getting difficult to function. Christian counseling helped me process the cause of my anxiety.
>
> I also dug into God's Word. Psalm 107:19–20 spoke volumes to my situation: "Then they cried to the Lord in their trouble, and he saved them from their distress. He sent out his word and healed them; he rescued them from the grave."
>
> I chose to believe and trust in the map I found in those two verses: cry out, trust Him to save me, and His Word would heal me . . . and I would be rescued from the grave.
>
> To begin, I got real with God about my pain. He already knew my heart, but crying out to Him helped me swallow my pride and acknowledge that He is capable of what I am not.
>
> Next, I chose to trust that He would save me. When I doubted the promises of His Word, I prayed that He would help me overcome my unbelief.
>
> Then I acknowledged the healing power of His Word. At first, I believed lies such as *I am unlovable* and *I will never be good enough.* These lies were much louder than the Scriptures I read. However, the more I repeated verses and altered my behavior to match His commands, belief began to manifest.

Last, I consented to a rescue from the grave. Honestly, I hadn't been eager for freedom because anxiety was a method of control. As long as I worried, I felt in control. If Christ was going to rescue me from the grave of anxiety, I would have to give up control and trust Him. That felt scary! But even scarier was the idea of continued physical and emotional death.

Choosing to trust Him involved a shift in my focus. I chose to see and accept the good in my life and to focus on what I could learn in this difficult season. Trusting Him meant choosing joy in the present over despair.[1]

It's been several years since Stephanie sat in her psychology class wearing a heart monitor. She's come to realize that although stress, anxiety, and fear will always be present, they don't have permission to infiltrate her heart and mind. Only God has permission to do that.

Are you in a battle with anxiety and fear today? Let God's promises remind you that He is your Healer, Protector, Rescuer, and Savior. He is your freedom from the grave of anxiety, doubt, and despair.

Dear Lord, help me to trust You, to consent to the healing power of Your Word, and to spend time in it believing and praying it for my life. Rescue me from my distress and from the grave of doubt and fear. Thank You for caring about me and setting me free. In Jesus' name, Amen.

When I say: I am battling fear and anxiety that won't go away.

God **says:** Cry out to Me when you are anxious and afraid. I will rescue you from the grave of despair.

Then they cried to the LORD in their trouble, and he saved them from their distress. He sent out his word and healed them; he rescued them from the grave. (Ps. 107:19–20)

44

Pursued

Now he had to go through Samaria . . . and Jesus, tired as he was from the journey, sat down by the well. It was about noon. When a Samaritan woman came to draw water, Jesus said to her, "Will you give me a drink?"

John 4:4, 6–7

She didn't know who this man was, and she couldn't help but wonder why He was talking to her, a Samaritan woman.

When He spoke, she heard gentleness in His voice; kindness and humility in His simple request for a drink. In His eyes, she saw acceptance, not judgment; love, not hate.

Many of us know her as "the Samaritan woman," but I like to call her Sam. It makes her feel more like the real woman she was. A woman who struggled with hurt, rejection, and loneliness.

Today's key verse says Jesus "had to go through Samaria." Yet theologians would tell us Jews considered Samaritans to be the scum of the earth and would do everything to avoid them. In fact, usually they would travel around Samaria—but not Jesus.

He *had* to go through Samaria. Could it be because He knew Sam would be there?

Typically women traveled together to the well in the cool of the day, escaping the heat of the sun since they would be carrying heavy water jars back to their homes. But Sam walked by herself during the hottest part of the day.

Many believe she went to the well at noon, under the scorching sun, to avoid the scorching pain of others' rejection and judgment. Sam had been married five times and now she was living with a man who wasn't her husband.

The weight of the water-filled jar in the heat must have been almost unbearable, but the weight of her neighbors' words, reminding her of her failed marriages, was more than she could take.

When Jesus met her, Sam was running an errand and running from those who knew of her failures, shame, and imperfections. Pursuing her with His perfect love, Jesus timed it so she would run into Him.

He initiated a conversation and asked her for the one thing she had to offer: water. It wasn't much, but it was a start.

Sam stopped and listened. She let Him speak words of assurance and acceptance into the broken, insecure, empty places of her heart.

In the same way Jesus intentionally pursued Sam in one of the loneliest parts of her day, He is there in the midst of your sometimes lonely, imperfect life. He is there when your disappointments and failures leave you empty and make you doubt your worth and purpose.

He is there when you're going through the motions, aware of what needs to be done but unaware of how you're going to do it all.

He is there during endless days filled with projects, diapers, or laundry, when you're wondering if you'll ever find meaning in the monotony.

He is there when you're criticizing yourself and questioning whether you have what it takes to be a godly woman.

He sees you. He notices all you do and He knows all that you long for. In fact, Jesus is the only One who can meet your deepest need to be known, accepted, and pursued simply because of who you are.

If you've ever doubted God's personal pursuit of you, let this truth sink in: *wherever you are, He wants to meet you there.* He is waiting for you to stop, come up close, and turn your heart to Him. You don't have to pretend things are fine when they aren't. He knows what is going on in your thoughts. Nothing could keep Him from wanting to be with you.

Today He is pursuing you, offering you the gift of His perfect love—love that is patient and kind, love that keeps no record of your wrongs, love that won't give up on you. Will you take time to stop and talk to Him, and then quiet your thoughts so you can listen to His?

Dear Lord, thank You for pursuing me. I want to know and rely on the love You have for me, and live in the security of it! When I feel afraid, insignificant, or alone, help me turn to You and remember You are there! In Jesus' name, Amen.

When I say: I'm not worth pursuing.

God **says:** I am here, pursuing you with My love each and every day.

I have loved you with an everlasting love; I have drawn you with unfailing kindness. (Jer. 31:3)

45

Changing Your Mind

Keep your mind clear, and be alert. Your opponent the devil is prowling around like a roaring lion as he looks for someone to devour. Be firm in the faith and resist him, knowing that other believers throughout the world are going through the same kind of suffering.

1 Peter 5:8–9 GW

You know that awful pit-in-the-stomach feeling when you let someone down? It's just what I felt after receiving an email from a friend telling me I'd dropped the ball on a project we were working on together.

I felt horrible for letting important details fall through the cracks. Immediately, critical thoughts of my own, and assumptions about her thoughts toward me, started running through my head.

I recognized, from past failures, that my imperfection is a place where Satan loves to prowl. He was ready to pounce on me with condemnation. But God's Word had taught me how to be aware of his schemes and ready to stand against them. In today's key verses, Peter tells us how:

Keep your mind clear, and be alert. Your opponent the devil is prowling around like a roaring lion as he looks for someone to devour. Be firm in the faith and resist him, knowing that other believers throughout the world are going through the same kind of suffering. (1 Pet. 5:8–9 GW)

I needed to keep my mind clear by asking Jesus to replace the clutter of critical thoughts with the clarity of His truth. This is crucial, because the battle begins in our minds and it's often precipitated by a fog of confusion and emotion.

I also knew I needed to be alert by listening to my thoughts. If my thoughts were against me, my feelings would be too. What we think determines how we feel, and our feelings often shape how we live.

Think → Feel → Live

I wrote down the facts of what had happened. For over three months, I had been through a very stressful season. A friend had died, we had adopted a baby from Ethiopia, my mom (who lives nearby) had been hospitalized with blood clots in her lungs, and my father (who lives states away) needed quadruple bypass heart surgery.

I was overwhelmed and exhausted physically, emotionally, mentally, and spiritually. I had cut back on a few things, but tried to push through and keep some commitments I'd made before the bottom fell out. Trying to not let others down had led to just that.

I pulled out my Bible and found promises to remind me that I need to do the best I can but then trust God with the rest. Here are a few verses I wrote in my journal that day:

- My flesh and my heart may fail, but God is the strength of my heart and my portion forever (Ps. 73:26).
- The LORD will accomplish what concerns me; Your lovingkindness, O LORD, is everlasting; Do not forsake the works of Your hands (Ps. 138:8 NASB).

• May the favor of the Lord our God rest on us; establish the work of our hands for us—yes, establish the work of our hands (Ps. 90:17).

Asking God to show me what I could learn from this hard lesson led to more cutbacks in my commitments and more delegating. After apologizing to my friend and explaining what had happened, I asked for forgiveness and she graciously gave it to me.

Letting God's promises change my mind by altering the way I thought completely transformed the way I felt. I was able to accept that, although I had done the best I could, my best wasn't good enough—but I still was.

Dear Jesus, sometimes my best isn't good enough. And other times I don't give my best in everything I do. Yet either way, You love me and I'm so glad. When hard things happen and I'm tempted to beat myself up, help me change my mind by changing the way I think, which will change the way I feel and live! In Your name, Amen.

When I say: I always let people down. I'm such a disappointment.

God **says:** Keep your mind clear of condemnation, and be alert. Your opponent the devil is prowling around like a lion looking to devour you with doubt.

Keep your mind clear, and be alert. Your opponent the devil is prowling around like a roaring lion as he looks for someone to devour. (1 Pet. 5:8 GW)

46

Shipwrecked

And we know that in all things God works for the good of those who love him, who have been called according to his purpose.

Romans 8:28

An undiagnosed illness had lingered for months when Micca started to feel rejected by God. The timing didn't make sense. She had been serving God in more ways than she could count. But now she was all but bedridden, week after week, unable to do life, let alone ministry.

Without warning, strong winds of sickness had come and ushered what felt like a storm into her life. Clouds hung overhead and before she knew it, Micca felt "shipwrecked."

One afternoon she was reading the story of Saul, a murderer, who had been transformed into Paul, a disciple of Christ. Even though Paul was a changed person, many rejected him because of his past reputation and lifestyle.

Not only that, but as Paul became fully devoted to serving Christ—sacrificing his education and his life, and remaining single so he could better serve the Lord—he was falsely accused, thrown into prison more than once, and shipwrecked on several occasions. *Doesn't that seem odd for a man called by God? Wouldn't God's favor protect him from such adversity?*

Perhaps you've been there too. Maybe you've been rejected by family, friends, or co-workers. Maybe you've been falsely accused. Maybe you're imprisoned by finances, or are being blown around by the consequences of someone else's sin.

It seems so unfair. You've tried to live right. You walk in obedience the best you can. You take God at His Word and trust in His promises. Shouldn't faith like this call for smooth sailing instead of stormy seas?

If we follow Paul's journey, we find God working through the rejection, the trials, the prison time, and the shipwrecks. Paul shared the gospel with the Pharisees through his rejection and imprisonment. People saw God's power at work when Paul survived the storms, when the snake bite didn't kill him, and when the jail shook—opening doors and loosing chains.

Paul didn't let his circumstances wreck him with a sense of rejection. He didn't allow self-pity and doubt to overtake him. Instead, we see in Acts 16:22–31 that after being stripped, beaten, severely flogged, and thrown in the inner cell of a prison with his feet in stocks, Paul prayed and sang hymns to God. And others around him were listening.

In fact, the power of God came in such a way that the prison guard begged Paul to tell him, "Sir, what must I do to be saved?" Paul replied, "Believe in the Lord Jesus" (vv. 30–31).

God kept His promise to work all things together for the good of this man who loved Him and was called according to His purposes. As Paul depended on God and trusted His faithfulness in the midst of adversity, many witnessed God's power and believed.

And the same is true for us. God doesn't waste our pain, our rejection, or our "shipwrecks." He uses them to bring about His plan—to position us so that others can see His transforming power at work in our lives and believe in the living God.[1]

When we are shipwrecked like Paul, we may feel put on hold, but actually God is holding us. And in the palm of His hand we are positioned to draw others to Jesus. Let's choose today to rise above our stormy seas to seek and praise Him, so God can use us to reflect His glory and His goodness in our lives.

Dear Lord, forgive me for wallowing in self-pity and rejection. I know You see the bigger picture and are working for my good and Your glory, bringing purpose in my pain. Strengthen me to arise from the wreckage of my storms so others will see that You are my help and my salvation. In Jesus' name, Amen.

When I say: My life is full of problems.

God **says:** I will use all things, even the hard things, for your good and My glory.

And we know that in all things God works for
the good of those who love him, who have been
called according to his purpose. (Rom. 8:28)

47

His Compassions Never Fail

Because of the LORD's great love we are not consumed, for his compassions never fail. They are new every morning; great is your faithfulness.

Lamentations 3:22–23

I was perusing the maternity clothes section in a small consignment store when my then-two-year-old son Joshua yanked my pants leg. Tears fell down his rosy cheeks as he pulled my hand and led me to his friend—a clothes mannequin.

Before I realized what he was doing, Joshua lifted her dress and said, "Look, Mommy," pointing to the metal rod shooting up her back for support. And then he whispered, "Ouch, that hurts."

Once I stopped blushing over the fact that we were looking up a mannequin's skirt, I was moved by Joshua's compassion for his new friend. I knelt in front of him to explain that she just needed some extra support but she was going to be okay.

Joshua's tender mercy was a picture of God's love to me—love that is full of compassion, love that shows concern not just with words but with actions. Joshua saw someone who was hurting—or so he thought—and he wanted to ease her pain.

His compassion reminded me of a familiar story Jesus told about a Samaritan man who was traveling one day and noticed an injured pedestrian who had been robbed, stripped of his clothes, and left for dead. Unlike others who ignored him as they passed by, this man saw the injured victim and was moved with compassion. He rushed to his side, bandaged his wounds, took him to an inn, and got him the care he needed.

Jesus told this story to show what *love in action* looks like. True to His nature, Jesus didn't just tell us to love, He showed us how to love. He loved us first.

He said, "Love sacrificially." Then He showed us what it looks like through His love for people who would betray Him, friends who would abandon Him, and crowds who would accuse Him. Yet He still chose to love unconditionally.

And then He demonstrated the ultimate act of *love in action* by sacrificing His life for ours. It was His never-failing compassion that moved His heart to act on our behalf—to rescue us.

Jesus came to our side. With an aching awareness of our injured hearts, our sin-wrecked lives, and our need for His forgiveness, He bent down and with outstretched hands offered to bandage our wounds and give us the care we needed.

The same compassion that moved God's heart over two thousand years ago moves His heart toward you today. No matter where you are or what you need, He offers healing for your hurts, comfort for your concerns, and rest for your wearied soul. Remember: His compassions never fail. They are new this very morning.

Dear Lord, thank You for seeing my greatest needs. When I fail or feel failed by others, remind this heart of mine that Your compassions never fail me. Thank You for loving me with

Your Words and Your actions. Help me do the same—love You and others with my life. In Jesus' name, Amen.

When I say: My needs are consuming.

God **says:** Let My compassions that are new every morning consume and comfort you.

Because of the LORD's great love we are not consumed,
for his compassions never fail. They are new every
morning; great is your faithfulness. (Lam. 3:22–23)

48

Peace-full

You will keep in perfect peace those whose minds are steadfast, because they trust in you.

Isaiah 26:3

I've always wanted to live in a home with a front porch that has rocking chairs on it. The funny thing is, sitting in a rocking chair makes me dizzy so I probably wouldn't even use them. But looking at rocking chairs makes me feel full of peace. And I long for a little more peace-full in my life, don't you?

Worry is the opposite of peace-full. Worry leaves us peace-less!

And, as Erma Bombeck once said, "Worry is like a rocking chair: it will give you something to do but it won't get you anywhere."[1] So, maybe I don't need those rocking chairs after all!

Worry really doesn't get us anywhere. Worry doesn't change anything. In fact, worry is a waste of time. Research shows that when it come to the things we worry about:

- 40 percent never happen
- 30 percent are in regard to unchangeable deeds of the past

- 12 percent focus on the opinions of others that cannot be controlled
- 10 percent center on personal health, which only worsens when we worry about it
- 8 percent concern real problems that we can influence[2]

If only 8 percent of our concerns are problems we can influence, why do we spend so much time worrying? I think it's because we have a hard time trusting God completely. And we have an enemy who wants us to doubt God's sovereignty and question His abilities.

He tries to convince us that we are the only ones who can change things, or that we need to worry about the people and problems in our lives because God's got bigger things to deal with such as economic downfalls and world peace. The war in the Middle East is much more important than our war with worry, right?

I think Jesus would disagree. He warned that our enemy is a thief who comes to steal, kill, and destroy (John 10:10). And one of his most effective robbery attempts is through a string of worrisome thoughts. That's why we need to recognize the enemy's schemes and realize the effects they have on us. An acronym that helps me remember how damaging worry can be is **Worry Only Robs Rest from You.**

- Worry robs you physically, leaving you exhausted.
- Worry robs you emotionally, leaving you anxious.
- Worry robs you mentally, leaving you scattered.
- Worry robs you spiritually, leaving you depleted.

And that's not all. When we feel exhausted, anxious, scattered, and depleted, we can start to doubt ourselves. We lack the energy we need to handle day-to-day events and can get overwhelmed with a sense of uncertainty, which leads to self-doubt. How often do you doubt you can manage your life, hear God clearly, or do all God has called you to do?

In the midst of our exhaustion and doubts, God promises to provide just what we need. Instead of letting worry rob us, let's take God up on His promise to keep our minds in perfect peace as we put our trust in Him:

- You make known to me the path of life; you will fill me with joy in your presence (Ps. 16:11).
- Whoever dwells in the shelter of the Most High will rest in the shadow of the Almighty. I will say of the Lord, "He is my refuge and my fortress, my God, in whom I trust" (Ps. 91:1–2).
- Though I walk in the midst of trouble, you preserve my life. You stretch out your hand against the anger of my foes; with your right hand you save me (Ps. 138:7).
- I have told you these things, so that in Me you may have [perfect] peace *and* confidence (John 16:33 AMP).

Jesus, when worry starts to rob me, help me stop and take hold of Your promises so I can live the peace-full life You offer me. Remind me that You are with me, holding me by my right hand and guiding me with Your counsel, keeping my heart in perfect peace as I put my trust in You! In Your name, Amen.

When I say: I feel overwhelmed.

God **says:** I will give you peace.

> You will keep in perfect peace those whose minds
> are steadfast, because they trust in you. (Isa. 26:3)

49

Remind Me Who I Am

One of them, the disciple whom Jesus loved, was reclining next to him.

John 13:23

When she was a freshman in high school, a boy gave her the nickname "Hips." Although Glynnis was thin, her shape was unlike the popular models of that time. And from that point on she was keenly and uncomfortably aware that she didn't have a "desirable" figure.

Glynnis told me the name Hips stuck in her mind for years, as she labeled herself unathletic and uncoordinated. "It didn't help that I got hit in the head at softball tryouts and was in the first cuts from the volleyball and basketball teams. I did get called back for a dancing spot in the school play, but went to the auditions in Levis 501 straight-leg jeans. Not exactly sure what I was thinking that day," she said.

But not too long ago, Glynnis discovered a truth in the book of John that reminded her of who she really is:

Unathletic isn't the only label I've given myself over the years. Some have been positive, others negative. Some were based on fact, yet others were based on emotion. The way I describe myself has a powerful effect on how I see myself . . . on my self-worth, value, and choices.

The New Testament tells of a disciple of Jesus who had an interesting definition for himself, one that seemed to impact his life as well. In the book of John, one of the disciples is described this way: *the one whom Jesus loved.*

Interestingly, this description is only found in the book of John, and scholars believe John the Apostle, the author of the book, was referring to himself.

For years I assumed this was a title the other disciples gave John. Perhaps they believed Jesus loved John more than the others. That wouldn't be uncommon, as siblings tend to have an unspoken understanding of who the favorite child is. But what if this title, this label, wasn't given by the others?

Recently it hit me that this identity—one loved by Jesus—was how *John* described *himself.* John was confident of Jesus' love, and this had a powerful effect on how he lived his life.

He didn't fear man's threats as he stood at the base of the cross, caring for Jesus' mother. Nor when he was among the first at the tomb, possibly facing bewildered and angry Roman soldiers. After the resurrection, John fearlessly preached the Good News alongside the others, and faced persecution and imprisonment.

John's confidence of Jesus' love emboldened him.

As I thought of all the descriptions I've given myself over the years, I realized that this one might be the most life-changing for me. It's one thing to identify myself as a Christian, as if it's a set of beliefs I adhere to. It's quite another to place myself in the "inner circle" because of Jesus' love for me. There's something that seems slightly presumptuous about that, and so it's safer to skirt on the edges of this relationship I have with Christ.

And yet when I dare to admit the possibility that Jesus might love me as much as He loved John . . . and that I too could call myself "one whom Jesus loves" . . . this changes who I am.[1]

You are the one Jesus loves, friend. You are invited to His inner circle of close friendship—today. And the only thing that can hold you back is you, and any faulty definitions you have of yourself.

Will you tear off the lies and the labels that have kept you from seeing yourself as Jesus sees you? Ask Him today to remind you who you are—the one He loves!

Dear heavenly Father, thank You for loving me unconditionally. Thank You for inviting me into Your intimate circle of friends—Your inner circle of love. Stitch this truth on my heart today. In Jesus' name, Amen.

When I say: I feel ugly and unwanted.

God **says:** You are My beloved.

You are precious and honored in my sight,
and . . . I love you. (Isa. 43:4)

50

Words for the Weary

The Sovereign Lord has given me his words of wisdom, so that I know how to comfort the weary. Morning by morning he wakens me and opens my understanding to his will.

Isaiah 50:4 NLT

---

*H*as someone ever said just what you needed to hear, and the words they spoke helped you see something valuable or unique about yourself that you had never seen before?

That's what happened between Jill and Leanne. They met when Jill was coaching a junior high basketball team and Leanne's thirteen-year-old daughter, Shelby, was on her team. Years later, when she was in high school, Shelby was seriously injured and Jill reached out to her with encouragement, prayers, and notes that spoke just the words Shelby needed to hear.

One day, Leanne sent a letter thanking Jill for the difference she was making in her daughter's life. She described the qualities of a great coach that she saw in Jill and called her a "bright light" that shined in many lives, including theirs.

Leanne didn't know that, months later, Jill would go home one night to an empty apartment, feeling weary and plagued with doubt, while questioning her purpose in life. Battling clinical depression and living under the weight of feeling worthless, Jill contemplated suicide. That night as she pondered her fate, she opened her journal and a piece of paper fell out. Opening the note, she read Leanne's words again.

God used Leanne's words to show Jill that she did have a purpose and that life was worth living. They were just the words she needed to hear.

When someone speaks encouragement into our hearts, the course of our lives can be changed forever. And when we believe in someone else, God uses us to build confidence and security in a heart that may have otherwise been paralyzed by doubt and insecurity.

Remember my friend Janet, who thanked me for words I'd penned from my heart to hers in a thank-you card? To me it was *only* a thank-you, but to her it was more. God touched her heart deeply through something I said. And in response, she encouraged me to write more than notes. Her encouragement was just what I needed to hear to have the courage to take the next step God had for me.

Perhaps there are words you need to hear today. If so, I would love to speak God's heart over you through His promises:

But you are a chosen [woman], a royal [priest], a holy [daughter], God's special possession, that you may declare the praises of him who called you out of darkness into his wonderful light. (1 Pet. 2:9)

Do not fear, for [He has] redeemed you; [He has] summoned you by name; you are [His]. (Isa. 43:1)

For [you] are God's masterpiece. He has created [you] anew in Christ Jesus, so [you] can do the good things he planned for [you] long ago. (Eph. 2:10 NLT)

In all these things [you] are more than [a] conqueror through him who loved [you]. (Rom. 8:37)

The Bible is filled with just the words our weary hearts need to hear. And when we read and believe God's promises for us, they settle into places in our souls that need to know we are loved . . . by Him and others.

I pray you receive and believe them today, and then ask Jesus how you might share them. Perhaps there is someone in your life who needs them now more than ever.

Dear Lord, I need Your encouragement each day. Lead me to promises in Your Word that will strengthen me when I'm weary and build me up when I feel torn down. Help me see and believe what You see in me, and then share it with others today. In Jesus' name, Amen.

When I say: I want to encourage others, but I don't know what to say.

God **says:** Listen with your heart and I will give you the words they need to hear.

> The Sovereign LORD has given me his words of wisdom, so that I know how to comfort the weary. Morning by morning he wakens me and opens my understanding to his will. (Isa. 50:4 NLT)

51

Because You Are His

For the LORD your God is living among you. He is a mighty savior. He will take delight in you with gladness. With his love, he will calm all your fears. He will rejoice over you with joyful songs.

Zephaniah 3:17 NLT

I sat up in bed so I could see the neon red numbers that told me it was three in the morning, time to feed the baby. But Andrew hadn't made a sound.

Wavering between panic and joy, I felt my way down the hall to his room and leaned over Andrew's crib. I listened for the sound of his breathing and carefully rested my hand on his tiny chest to feel the gentle rhythm of its rising and falling.

Moonlight slipped through the blinds, helping me see he was perfectly fine. Most sane moms would have gone back to bed, but not me. I stood there for a while just delighting in my child.

The love and joy I felt at that moment were almost overwhelming. *How could I love someone so much?* My heart longed just to be with this little guy who set my days in motion with his cries and smiles.

Andrew developed a routine of sleeping through the night soon after, yet I'd still tiptoe into his room just to watch him sleep.

Both of my sons are teenagers now, but sometimes I still sneak into their rooms to pray over them and watch them while they are sleeping. They don't have to be doing anything to make me feel proud or happy. In fact, they may have even driven me to my wit's end that day, but I delight in them because they are mine.

God feels the exact same way about you. He loves to be with you and watch over you. Not because you are doing anything for Him, but simply because you are His. You might have even disappointed Him that day, but it doesn't change how He feels about you.

He delights greatly in you. And with His love, He is there today to quiet your fears, insecurities, and doubts. I have a feeling the joy-filled songs He sings over you are written just for you, describing the beautiful woman He's created you to be while gently leading your heart to know and rely on His love more and more each day.

What a great reminder for days when nothing's going right, when you feel like the whole world is against you and nobody understands what you're going through.

If you're having one of those days or weeks, I hope you'll remember the love of a mother watching her child sleeping. And remember that your heavenly Father loves and delights in you even more than that—all because you are His!

Dear Lord, thank You for the reminder that You are always with me and that You love to watch over me, every minute of every day—even while I am sleeping! Help me to completely believe the truth about Your love toward me. In Jesus' name, Amen.

When I say: No one is there for me.

God **says:** I am here for you, watching over you each day.

> For the LORD your God is living among you. He is a
> mighty savior. He will take delight in you with glad-
> ness. With his love, he will calm all your fears. He will
> rejoice over you with joyful songs. (Zeph. 3:17 NLT)

52

Failing Forward

Though the righteous fall seven times, they rise again.

Proverbs 24:16

---

*F*ailure is painful and embarrassing. Sometimes it makes me want to give up—mainly on myself. But God's been teaching me a lot about failure lately, reminding me that I am a work in progress—a woman who is *becoming* all He created her to be.

A woman who is growing.

A woman who is getting better at following God's ways.

A woman who is learning to *fail forward* even when failure sets me back.

Failing forward . . . after I forget a commitment I made to a friend.

Failing forward . . . after I shoot harsh words across the room to "shush" my child.

Failing forward . . . after I criticize my husband and realize I failed to honor my man, again.

Failing forward . . . after being "too busy" to be with my mom who stopped by unexpectedly.

Don't we all struggle with feeling like a failure in one area of our lives or another? For some, it's our past. Our childhood was not what we hoped it would be. Or we've made devastating choices we wish we could erase. Maybe it's our career. We were overlooked for a promotion at work or a position at church.

Maybe we're not married yet, and that feels like a failure as everyone around us has moved on to the next phase of life. Or we can't have children and wonder if God thinks we're just not cut out for parenthood.

Sometimes it's not the big things—it's the smaller, everyday things. How often do you hear doubt whisper, *You're such a failure*, when you make a dumb mistake, say something you regret, argue with or dishonor someone you love, let a friend down, or fall into a pattern of sin?

How often do you beat yourself up, saying things like, *I always do that. I'll never change.* Today's key verse has helped me move forward even when sin sets me back with regret, guilt, fear, and shame. It says, "Though the righteous fall seven times, they rise again" (Prov. 24:16).

Take a minute to read it again and notice how it says *the righteous will fall.* Yes, even those of us who have received the gift of Christ's righteousness and redemption will fail and feel like we've fallen down. But we were never intended to stay down.

Failure produces wisdom when we ask for it and maturity when we learn from it. And although it seems contradictory, failure can help us become the confident women God created us to be by making us stronger and better—if we *fail forward* and go to God for help.

So next time you fail, let it become a catalyst that leads you to Jesus and the Bible for wisdom and biblical perspective. Then look for ways to apply God's truths in the relationship, responsibility, or role you failed in by apologizing, redoing your work with more attention to detail, or asking for a do-over and communicating in a more gracious way.

Remember, although you may not be who you want to be, you are not who you used to be, and you get that much closer to who you are meant to be every time you *fail forward.*

Dear Lord, I am so thankful that with Your help I can fail forward! I don't have to see my setbacks as a step back. In fact, they can lead me forward if I let them. Today, I will take Your hand and trust Your heart as You use my failures to help me become the woman You created me to be. In Jesus' name, Amen.

When I say: I feel like such a failure.

God **says:** Choose to fail forward by learning and growing from your failures.

> Though the righteous fall seven times,
> they rise again. (Prov. 24:16)

53

Compelled by Love Alone

*Long before he laid down earth's foundations, he had us
in mind, had settled on us as the focus of his love, to be
made whole and holy by his love.*

Ephesians 1:4 Message

I'd been trying to connect with my son's teacher to give
her a thank-you gift and a wedding gift before the school
year ended. She had invested her prayers and her love in my son,
which created a love for her in my heart.

So I was determined to personally deliver the gifts before she
got married and moved away. I went by her classroom twice, but
missed her both times. We then played email tag all summer while
two beautiful boxes sat in my van.

Every time I saw them, a deep desire washed over me: I desperately wanted to get the gifts to her, personally tell her how much
she meant to me, and thank her for all she had done to impact my
child's life that year.

Finally, we connected on the phone the day before her move. She
gave me directions and said to call when we got there. However,

when we arrived at her apartment building, I realized I'd forgotten her phone number. And I didn't have her apartment number either. There we sat in front of a three-story building with twenty-four apartments to choose from.

So, what's a desperately determined woman to do? Get her husband, two sons, and their friend to go door-to-door in search of the teacher, while she drives around the parking lot in case the teacher comes out of a different building.

My husband thought I'd lost my mind. But he knew I was hormonal and didn't want to risk questioning my "brilliant" plan. When the guys couldn't find her, I got out and started knocking. Still no teacher.

Next, I suggested we search the parking lot for cars filled with contents resembling the belongings of a fourth grade teacher who is getting married (oh yes I did). After five minutes, I admitted my plan wasn't working.

The next day I told my co-workers about my desperate search. Some laughed, a few confessed to their own acts of desperation, but one reminded me that Jesus was just as determined to find us! Compelled by love alone, He wanted to personally deliver the gift of His life and His love to us!

Perhaps you've been wondering if you matter much to God. You do! So much that He left the riches of heaven and wrapped Himself in the rags of earth to come to you. Ephesians 1:4 reminds us that "Long before he laid down earth's foundations, he had [you] in mind, had settled on [you] as the focus of his love, to be made whole and holy by his love" (Message).

Jesus could have sent His gift through some other means, but He was determined to come to us personally to give the gift of His love, the gift of His life. A gift that should remind us each and every day how much we mean to Him.

God, thank You for being so determined to pursue me. Thinking about Your love compelling You to come to me personally to give me the gift of life and the gift of Your love takes my breath away. I cherish Your amazing grace that never gives up on me! In Jesus' name, Amen.

When I say: No one sees me.

God **says:** I see you. You are the focus of My love.

Long before he laid down earth's foundations, he had [me] in mind, had settled on [me] as the focus of his love, to be made whole and holy by his love. (Eph. 1:4 Message)

54

Mistaken Identity

Whoever belongs to God hears what God says.

John 8:47

Karen poured a cup of coffee and logged on to her laptop to peek at a friend's Facebook page.

When she tried hopping over to see her friend's latest pictures, she couldn't get her name to appear in the search bar. Feeling puzzled, she wondered why it wasn't working. Glancing at the top of the screen, she then realized she wasn't logged in to her own account. Her son had forgotten to sign off, so she was logged in as him instead.

Karen couldn't get where she wanted to go because she had mistaken her identity. She shared what God showed her as a result of her mistake:

> With a quick click of a mouse I switched accounts and used Facebook as "me." Under the right identity I was free to view pages, leave comments with ease, and get where I wanted to go.

Sometimes in life we encounter the same issue—we don't realize we have mistaken our identity. We log in to our day and encounter wrong thinking that makes us forget who we really are. This may happen when a voice from our past or our own negative self-talk urges us to forget our identity in Christ. When we do, we're blocked by doubt and can't get where God is calling us to go: to a life lived with our security and value rooted deep in His thoughts toward us.

Instead we hear:

"You can't do that. You aren't good enough."

"You'll never change."

"Why can't you be more like your sister?"

"If only you were more _____ instead of so _____."

When statements of self-doubt seem to scream and discouragement sets in, we need to log out of the lies we believe and log in to God's truth. It's the only way we will know and live in our true identity so that we can navigate our lives according to God's Word.

Here are some truths we can tell ourselves to remember who we are:

I am the daughter of the Most High God.

I am loved, redeemed, and renewed.

I am chosen, blameless, and holy.

I was bought at a great price.

God knows me thoroughly and yet loves me completely.

He has plans for my future that include hope, not harm; blessings, not banishment.

I belong to Him.[1]

As John 8:47 reminds us, it's imperative that we listen to God's Word and let it replace our false and destructive thoughts—even if we think they are true. Replacing our negative internal dialogue with Scripture is the only way we can remember who we are as children of God.

Because we "belong to God," let's make a commitment to hear what He says and soak in the power of His promises each day. As we log in to His truths, no longer will we mistake our identity. Instead, we'll know the confident reality of who we are in Christ.

Jesus, when I am tempted to think of myself in a way that isn't healthy or true, please remind me that I am Yours. In You I have security, significance, acceptance, belonging, value, and purpose. In Your name I pray, Amen.

When I say: It's hard to believe God's promises are true for me.

God **says:** Choose to live in the security of My promises, no matter what your feelings tell you.

Blessed is she who has believed that the Lord would fulfill his promises to her! (Luke 1:45)

55

Surrender

They will be called oaks of righteousness, a planting of the LORD *for the display of his splendor.*

Isaiah 61:3

Mary Ann had believed in me, invested in me, and encouraged me. She'd also prayed for me and stood beside me, helping me overcome fears and doubts as I followed God's call into ministry.

Now my dearest friend, who was also our church's women's ministry director, was moving hours away and would no longer be present in my everyday life to cheer me.

Tears streamed down my cheeks as I whispered, "How am I going to make it without her, God?"

Trying to find a distraction for my despair, I decided to tackle yard work. As I headed outside, I noticed a rosebush the previous homeowner had planted. It was in full bloom, displaying its splendor through gorgeous pink blossoms across the center of our split rail fence.

How did that happen? I wondered. I had not done anything to care for it.

I remembered seeing rose fertilizer in our shed, so I grabbed some and took it over to the fence. Pulling the weeds away from the bush's base so the plant food could sink into the soil, I noticed the root ball had four sections.

Should I leave the sections all together or divide and place them at different posts on the fence? I wondered.

If I moved them to separate posts, their vines could eventually connect and create a blanket of pink across the whole fence. With that image in mind, I knelt down and pressed my hands into the dirt to find the right places to separate the root ball.

At that moment, God whispered to my heart that the rosebush was a picture of what He was doing with the women's ministry I loved. Each of us serving on the team had been carefully planted in our giftedness, nurtured and encouraged through prayer, equipped through training, and fertilized by opportunities to serve. And we had become a display of God's splendor.

Yet, like this rosebush, we had reached the fullness of His glory in our current soil. We were ready to be divided so that His glory would be more fully displayed as He planted each of us uniquely and individually in new places of ministry.

My heart sank. *Would there be more pruning, more changes? More breaking up of what had taken years to establish?* That was nowhere in my hopes and plans!

Isn't it painful when God allows our dreams to be shattered, our relationships to be separated, and our fears to be realized?

I doubted what God was doing. I doubted any good could come from such loss. I doubted I could make it through the pain. Yet, as I imagined God's glory being more fully displayed, my heart settled into a place of surrender. It wasn't my plan, but if it was for His glory wasn't that what I wanted? Would I trust Him to ease my sorrow and bring something good from it?

That afternoon I knelt on holy ground in front of my rose-bush and surrendered the broken dreams in my heart. Even if it meant letting go of what I loved so deeply, it would be worth it if others would see God more fully in my life and eventually in my ministry.

Are you in a season of being uprooted? Has God rearranged your dreams and your future? Is He asking you to surrender your plans for His?

Jesus' life and death display God's promise to turn our despair into divine purpose if we will depend on and trust in Him.

God took my doubts and sorrow and used them to draw me into deeper dependence on Him. And in that season of replanting, He brought me to a new place of security that was based on the courage I found in Him.

My year of surrender also became a display of His splendor as those around me noticed His peace replacing my sadness and His hope replacing my despair.

As you courageously trust God's heart, ask Him to reveal Himself to you and then let Him reveal Himself through you. Hold your dreams and plans up to Jesus in surrender, and watch your life become a display of His splendor.

Lord, remind my heart of the transforming work You do—revealing Your splendor through my surrender—as I rely on Your love and strength. I put my trust in Your plans today. In Jesus' name, Amen.

When I say: I'm afraid to let go.

God **says:** You can trust My heart. Watch and see how My splendor will be displayed in your surrender.

They will be called oaks of righteousness, a planting of the LORD for the display of his splendor. (Isa. 61:3)

56

Talking Trash or Talking Truth?

So do not throw away your confidence; it will be richly re-
warded. You need to persevere so that when you have done
the will of God, you will receive what he has promised.

Hebrews 10:35–36

I was wiping down our kitchen countertops one afternoon
when I found a little rubber thingy. I didn't know what it
was, so I threw it away. But as soon as I tossed it in the trash can,
I remembered it was the power button for our TV remote control.

Digging through layers of dirty paper plates, sticky plastic cups,
and other stinky items, I finally found the tiny rubber button. As
I retrieved the item I had so quickly thrown away, I sensed God
telling me that's how easily I throw away my confidence—without
recognizing it.

It's usually very subtle. Just hours earlier, I'd cried out to God
from a place of defeat and doubt, telling Him how impossible it
was for me to finish a huge writing project I had, and how stupid
it was for me to commit to something I couldn't do. I hated the
pendulum swing between my dreams and my realities.

As I stood there with the power button in my hand, I realized God was trying to show me what I had been throwing away for years. Every time I said *God, I can't do this. I'm not smart enough. My faith is too weak. My life is a mess. I'll never change*, I threw away my confidence.

And every time I threw away my confidence, I threw away the power that could be mine if I chose to live in the security of God's promises instead of the insecurity of my doubts.

Do you ever question your abilities, your competency, or your worth? How often do you talk trash to your heart by agreeing with the whispers of self-doubt and throwing away confidence that should be yours as a child of God?

The next time you're tempted to throw away your confidence, ask Jesus to help you identify the doubt you are believing, write it down on a piece of paper, and trash that insecurity instead.

When self-doubt whispers, *I can't do that. I'm going to fail and look foolish*, trash that lie and tell yourself this truth: "The Lord is my helper, I will not be afraid. What can mere mortals do to me?" (Heb. 13:6).

When self-doubt whispers, *I'll never change*, trash that lie and tell yourself this truth: "*For I am* confident of this very thing, that He who began a good work in [me] will perfect it until the day of Christ Jesus" (Phil. 1:6 NASB).

When self-doubt whispers, *This is too hard for me. I don't have what it takes*, trash that lie and tell yourself this truth: "No, in all these things [I am] more than [a conqueror] through him who loved [me]" (Rom. 8:37).

Lord, help me recognize when I throw away my confidence and remind me to throw away my insecurities instead. I choose to persevere, knowing that my faith will be richly rewarded, and when I have done the will of God, by believing

You, I will receive what You have promised—a confident heart in Christ! In His name I pray, Amen.

When I say: I'm not smart enough. My faith is too weak. I'll never change.

God **says:** Don't throw away your confidence. Persevere in faith by replacing your doubts with the power of My promises.

> So do not throw away your confidence; it will be richly rewarded. You need to persevere so that when you have done the will of God, you will receive what he has promised. (Heb. 10:35–36)

57

I'm beyond Hurt

Though I walk in the midst of trouble, you preserve my life. You stretch out your hand against the anger of my foes; with your right hand you save me.

Psalm 138:7

I'm beyond hurt.
I'm beyond confused.
I'm beyond stressed.
I'm beyond tired . . . physically, emotionally, and mentally.

My friend Melissa wrote these words in her journal one morning. She knew she could keep going, but she also knew that when she felt this way, she had a choice: she could let her thoughts ride the waves of her crashing emotions, or she could anchor her thoughts to the solid truth of God's promises. She said:

I have to be intentional to focus on a different set of "beyond" statements or I quickly find myself sinking. I know this from experience. Even if the "beyond" statements above are true, there are others that are also true.

I am beyond blessed: *From the fullness of his grace we have all received one blessing after another.* John 1:16

I am beyond strong: *Have I not commanded you? Be strong and courageous. Do not be afraid; do not be discouraged, for the* LORD *your God will be with you wherever you go.* Joshua 1:9

I am beyond secure: *Peace I leave with you; my peace I give you. I do not give to you as the world gives. Do not let your hearts be troubled and do not be afraid.* John 14:27

I am beyond safe: *Though I walk in the midst of trouble, you preserve my life; you stretch out your hand against the anger of my foes, with your right hand you save me.* Psalm 138:7

I am beyond hopeful: *"For I know the plans I have for you," declares the* LORD, *"plans to prosper you and not to harm you, plans to give you hope and a future."* Jeremiah 29:11

I am beyond loved: *But I trust in your unfailing love; my heart rejoices in your salvation.* Psalm 13:5

I am beyond valued: *For God so loved the world that he gave his one and only Son, that whoever believes in him shall not perish but have eternal life.* John 3:16

I am beyond forgiven: *Then Jesus said to her, "Your sins are forgiven."* Luke 7:48

I am beyond found: *Suppose one of you has a hundred sheep and loses one of them. Doesn't he leave the ninety-nine in the open country and go after the lost sheep until he finds it? And when he finds it, he joyfully puts it on his shoulders and goes home. Then he calls his friends and neighbors together and says, "Rejoice with me; I have found my lost sheep."* Luke 15:4–6

I am beyond complete: *So you also are complete through your union with Christ, who is the head over every ruler and authority.* Colossians 2:10 NLT

We can't trust our feelings, or even circumstances, to tell us how we are. They change like the wind. Up one moment and easily shot down the next. But God's Word never changes. His unmoving truths go beyond our emotions and the circumstances our day holds to anchor us in hope.

Some days, weeks, or even seasons of life are discouraging and we can't see beyond the pain, hurt, and stress. Searching God's Word to find His view of our circumstances and of us lifts our eyes off the problems and onto Him.[1]

Today, let's ask God to lead us beyond our hurts to our ultimate source of hope: His truth and encouragement!

Dear Lord, thank You for recording Your Word for me to reflect on and find truth in. Thank You for giving hope and peace beyond my feelings and circumstances. In Jesus' name, Amen.

When I say: I'm beyond hurt.

God **says:** But you are not beyond My reach. Let Me walk with you through these troubles and help you today.

Though [you] walk in the midst of trouble, [I] preserve [your] life; [I] stretch out [My] hand against the anger of [your] foes, with [My] right hand [I] save [you]. (Ps. 138:7)

58

He Bends Down

Because he bends down to listen, I will pray as long as I have breath!

Psalm 116:2 NLT

---

*I*t had been a hard day, running too many errands with two small children. My three-year-old didn't understand why we couldn't buy every toy his tiny hands could touch. And he kept getting in and out of the grocery cart, and whining when I tried to stop him.

I was not a happy mama and wondered how all the other moms in the store seemed to know what they were doing.

Their children listened when they told them *no*, and they wore cute matching outfits too. I wondered how in the world those women pulled it off with a smile. I could barely get a shower, get my kids dressed, and get us out the door before lunch.

When we got home that afternoon, I went looking for pink construction paper so I could write "I QUIT" on it and turn in my "pink slip" to JJ when he came home from work. I was tired of feeling like such a failure as a mom.

When I couldn't find pink paper, I decided to pull out my journal. Filling blank pages with scribbled thoughts, I wrote:

I hate who I have become. I'm such a horrible mom. Why didn't someone tell me how hard this was going to be? I'm frustrated with my kids and myself. I have no patience and I don't know what I am doing! I feel guilty all the time. I couldn't wait to be a mom and now I want to quit.

Just as I finished writing that sentence, I sensed God whispering to me: *Renee, you are so critical of yourself. You focus on your mistakes and beat yourself up with accusation and condemnation. Those are not My thoughts.*

That afternoon, I fell on my knees before God and choked out the words, "I can't do this."

And in that place of surrender, His peace came over me. His gentleness calmed my nerves. It felt like God bent down before me to listen, and He spoke to my heart: *You are right, Renee. In your strength and through your perspective, you can't do this. But with My promises, My presence, and My power—all things are possible. I will help you.*

Looking back on that day, I'm reminded of our key verse in Psalm 116:2, "Because he bends down to listen, I will pray as long as I have breath!" (NLT).

When we acknowledge that on our own we are a mess, God rushes to our side to help us. He bends down to show us that with His help, wisdom, and guidance, we can become the confident women He created us to be!

Dear Lord, I need Your shield of victory to protect me from discouragement. I pray that You would extend Your right hand to sustain me, Your grace to strengthen me, and Your wisdom to lead me. Thank You for Jesus, who stooped down to make me great because of Your great love for me. Today, I want to find a new starting place with You. In Jesus' name, Amen.

When I say: I can't do this.

God **says:** You can do all things through Christ who gives you strength. Keep praying and depending on Me for help.

> I can do all this through him who
> gives me strength. (Phil. 4:13)

59

Turning Worry into Worship

Come, let us bow down in worship, let us kneel before the LORD *our Maker.*

Psalm 95:6

---

*Y*esterday, the number of things I had to get done outnumbered the hours in my day! When I woke up, I knew I had a decision to make. I didn't want to worry about the "hows and whens" of my week. I wanted to be able to focus on one thing at a time and not be stressed out.

But focusing is not a natural gift for me. I tend to think about a lot of different things all at once. And instead of just thinking about them, I start worrying about them too.

However, there are many times when I don't even realize I'm worried. God wired my mind to think a lot, so I am used to the constant flurry of motion in my brain. Worry will slowly start to creep in, and before I know it there's a stirring in my heart, my neck gets tense, my mind won't shift gears, and little concerns kick into full-blown worries.

I know I should pray, but too often insead of talking to Jesus I will just start talking to myself in my head, until my accumulation of thoughts become consuming concerns.

But yesterday morning, I decided I was going to make my worries work for me. First, I made a list of my concerns and tasks, and told God I needed His help. To that list, I added descriptions of what I felt like I needed to do or attributes I needed to have—such as being focused, organized, patient, and compassionate.

Then I made a list of God's character traits that I needed Him to be for me—and thanked Him for being the very things I needed: able, loving, patient, wise, organized, focused, compassionate . . . and the list went on and on.

As I did this, His peace came over me. A peace that surpassed my understanding. A peace that calmed my anxious heart.

It's a peace that comes whenever I position my heart to worship instead of worry.

I found this way of making worry work for me when I started following the apostle Paul's prescription for peace in Philippians 4:6–7, where he tells us: "Don't worry about anything; instead, pray about everything. Tell God what you need and thank him for all he has done. Then you will experience God's peace, which exceeds anything we can understand. His peace will guard your hearts and minds as you live in Christ Jesus" (NLT). The first time I read his words, I thought it sounded so doable. Yet I wondered why it was so hard.

I think it's because Satan whispers the opposite. He tells us, "Don't be calm about anything; instead, worry about everything. Tell God what He should do. Then take control if He doesn't listen." And when we listen to those whispers, our concerns become consuming, almost like acid in our hearts, eroding our confidence with worry and doubt.

Instead of worrying, let's start worshiping by following God's promise for peace. When we feel overwhelmed by life this week, let's commit to:

- **Stop worrying.** Press the pause button on our consuming concerns.
- **Start praying.** Talk to God about all we're doing. Ask if there's anything we need to cut back so we can seek Him as much as we serve Him and others.
- **Keep thanking God.** Thank God for what He's done in the past and will do in the future. This act of worship helps us remember how good He is at being God.

We will always have days that are overwhelming and worries that threaten to steal our focus. When that happens, let's remember to *stop worrying*, *start praying*, and *keep thanking God* for how much He cares about us as we cast our cares upon Him.

Lord, when my concerns consume me, remind me to take my eyes off my worries and focus on worshiping You instead. Help me kneel down in my heart and worship You, my Maker, by remembering that You are the One who can accomplish all that concerns me. In Jesus' name, Amen.

When I say: I can't stop worrying.

God **says:** Take your eyes off your worries and focus on worshiping Me instead, remembering that I can accomplish all that concerns you.

Don't worry about anything; instead, pray
about everything. (Phil. 4:6 NLT)

60

A Lifetime Heart Warranty

For no matter how many promises God has made, they are "Yes" in Christ. . . . Now it is God who makes both us and you stand firm in Christ. He anointed us, set his seal of ownership on us, and put his Spirit in our hearts as a deposit, guaranteeing what is to come.

2 Corinthians 1:20–22

———

Why did we opt for this stress? I wondered. A houseful of men hammering, banging, scraping, and making minor repairs for two days was about to send my "need-for-peace-and-quiet" personality over the edge.

I knew I should be thankful. The work was being done at no charge under our one-year home warranty. But now I wished we had waited until things were *really* broken. Instead we opted for inconvenience and lots of noise, knowing that our "brokenness" would then be fixed for free.

Hoping a little bit of nature might settle my nerves and help my attitude, I headed out for a morning walk before the workers showed up again. Praying for peace and a new perspective, I asked God to help me create a gratitude list.

I thanked Him for helping us notice a dripping toilet upstairs, a small gap behind our countertop, rippled carpet in my son's room, and hairline fractures in our kitchen and laundry room tiles. All of which we had missed until just before our warranty expired.

After my "mental tour" of our house, I asked Jesus to show me areas of my heart that needed some fixing too. I knew something was wrong, but I didn't know why I was so anxious and frustrated about our house repairs.

As I listened quietly to my thoughts, the Holy Spirit reminded me of hurt from a difficult conversation I'd had that week. Disappointment and broken trust from one of my kids' disobedience was also taking a toll on me. And God showed me the heavy weight of concern I was carrying for a friend who had just found out her husband committed adultery, and another friend who was recently diagnosed with cancer.

Taking a deep breath, I wondered if He had anything more to show me. That's when Jesus reminded me that, like my home warranty (but so much better), He offers me a lifetime heart warranty with unlimited repairs. And although it's hard and often inconvenient, it's something I need every day, and it's totally free.

As I let that truth wash over my worn-out emotions, His comfort came. His Spirit ministered to mine as I processed my hurts, doubts, concerns, and chaos with Him. I remembered today's promise: His Spirit is in me and He makes me stand firm—even when my feelings are frayed and my mind is frazzled.

Each day, Jesus is there to work on or mend the broken places in our relationships and in our hearts. We don't have to wait for a scheduled walk-through. We don't have to make a list and coordinate any appointments, or even be at home for Him to do the work.

As you continue your journey of living with a confident heart in Christ, I pray that you will keep *relying on* and *living in* the power of God's promises knowing that He has set His seal of ownership on you—His lifetime heart warranty, guaranteeing what is to come!

Dear Lord, thank You for always being there for me, and for promising to make me new, even when I feel worn out, stressed, and like I'm falling apart sometimes. I pray You would help me see how You are working in my life, fulfilling Your promises as I put my hope in You. In Jesus' name, Amen.

When I say: I'm a mess. How can God keep His promises to me?

God **says:** My promises have no conditions. You have a lifetime warranty with Me.

> For no matter how many promises God has made, they are "Yes" in Christ . . . Now it is God who makes both us and you stand firm in Christ. He anointed us, set his seal of ownership on us, and put his Spirit in our hearts as a deposit, guaranteeing what is to come. (2 Cor. 1:20–22)

Appendix A

Personality Summary

Phlegmatic: Desires PEACE

Needs times of quiet, reduced stress, feeling of worth, respect

Strengths	Relational Challenges
Calm	Stubborn
Adds balance	Uninvolved
Witty	Procrastinates
Low-key	Unenthusiastic
Considerate	Hard to motivate
Reliable	Denial
Makes peace	Careless

Choleric: Desires CONTROL

Needs appreciation for achievements, opportunity for leadership, participation in decisions

Strengths	Relational Challenges
Problem solver	Opinionated
Decisive	Workaholic tendency
Natural leader	Usurps authority
Good organizer	Insensitive

Choleric: Desires CONTROL

Needs appreciation for achievements, opportunity for leadership, participation in decisions

Strengths	Relational Challenges
Task oriented	Arrogant
High energy	Manipulative
Excels in crisis	Has a hard time admitting her faults
Confident	

Sanguine: Desires FUN

Needs interaction, affection, approval, attention

Strengths	Relational Challenges
Loves people	Emotional
Friendly	Dislikes schedules
Exciting	Makes excuses
Humorous	Gets bored easily
Charming	Loses track of time
Creative	Takes on too much
Thrives on activity	Easily distracted
Great storyteller	

Melancholy: Desires PERFECTION

Needs understanding, stability, support, space, silence

Strengths	Relational Challenges
Works well alone	Easily depressed
Planner	Lacks spontaneity
Organized	Naively idealistic
Accurate	Thrifty to extremes
Intuitive	Doesn't do well under pressure
Fair	Perfectionist
Creative	Hard to please
Empathetic	Discontent
Good with numbers	

Appendix B

When You Say, God Says

When I Say	God Says	Powerful Promises
My doubts won't go away.	I am calling you out of the darkness. Turn toward the light and truth of what I say about you.	You are a chosen [woman], a royal [priest], a holy [daughter], God's special possession, that you may declare the praises of him who called you out of the darkness into his wonderful light. (1 Pet. 2:9)
Why do I still struggle with self-doubt?	It takes time to overcome lifelong doubt. Let's walk through the process of finding your confidence through your relationship with Me.	But blessed is the one who trusts in the LORD, whose confidence is in him. (Jer. 17:7)
My life is too hard.	I am with you in the middle of these trials. I will neither leave you nor forsake you.	I will be with [you] in trouble, I will deliver [you] and honor [you]. (Ps. 91:15)
I can't get past my past.	Let Me help you heal from your past so it doesn't hinder the plans I have for your future. I want to do a new thing in you.	Forget the former things; do not dwell on the past. See, I am doing a new thing! Now it springs up; do you not perceive it? I am making a way in the wilderness and streams in the wasteland. (Isa. 43:18–19)

When I Say	God Says	Powerful Promises
I am afraid to trust God.	Spend time with Me and get to know My heart by depending on Me a little more each day.	Those who know your name trust you, O LORD, because you have never deserted those who seek your help. (Ps. 9:10 GW)
I'm afraid to do what God is calling me to do.	I have not given you a spirit of fear.	For God has not given us a spirit of fear and timidity, but of power, love, and self-discipline. (2 Tim. 1:7 NLT)
Everything is going wrong in my life.	Focus on Me instead of your circumstances, remembering how I've taken care of you before.	Praise the LORD, my soul; all my inmost being, praise his holy name. Praise the LORD, my soul, and forget not all his benefits. (Ps. 103:1–2)
I don't like who I am or how I do things.	I made you, and I love you just the way you are!	For [you] are God's handiwork, created in Christ Jesus to do good works, which God prepared in advance for [you] to do. (Eph. 2:10)
I feel so flawed and imperfect.	Because My love for you is perfect, you don't have to be.	Being confident of this, that he who began a good work in you will carry it on to completion until the day of Christ Jesus. (Phil. 1:6)
I'm fine (although I'm *really* not).	You don't have to pretend. My power is perfected in your weakness, and others want to know you're not perfect.	"My grace is sufficient for you, for power is perfected in weakness." Most gladly, therefore, I will rather boast about my weaknesses, so that the power of Christ may dwell in me. (2 Cor. 12:9 NASB)
I just want to quit.	Don't give in and let discouragement win.	[You] do not belong to those who shrink back and are destroyed, but to those who have faith and are saved. (Heb. 10:39)
I feel so ashamed and condemned.	Shame is from the evil one. I will never condemn you.	Therefore, there is now no condemnation for those who are in Christ Jesus. (Rom. 8:1)
I don't want to be a burden on others.	Let those close to you encourage, pray for, and comfort you in times of need.	Never stop praying, especially for others. Always pray by the power of the Spirit. Stay alert and keep praying for God's people. (Eph. 6:18 CEV)

When I Say	God Says	Powerful Promises
I haven't got time to deal with my pain.	If we don't process the pain from your yesterdays, it will creep into your todays and keep you from experiencing all I have for your tomorrows.	The Lord will surely comfort [you] and will look with compassion on all [your] ruins; he will make [your] deserts like Eden, [your] wastelands like the garden of the Lord. (Isa. 51:3)
I don't deserve another chance.	I will remember your sins no more.	For I will be merciful to [your] iniquities, and I will remember [your] sins no more. (Heb. 8:12 NASB)
I don't know what to say when I pray.	Just talk to Me and pray through My promises today.	This is the confidence which we have before Him, that, if we ask anything according to His will, He hears us. (1 John 5:14 NASB)
My life is too busy. I don't have time to spend with God.	Come with Me to a quiet place and get some rest for your heart, mind, and soul.	Then, because so many people were coming and going that they did not even have a chance to eat, he said to them, "Come with me by yourselves to a quiet place and get some rest." (Mark 6:31)
I'm constantly messing up.	Your mistakes don't define you, but you can let them refine you.	The steps of a man are established by the LORD, and He delights in his way. When he falls, he will not be hurled headlong, because the LORD is the One who holds his hand. (Ps. 37:23–24 NASB)
I can't forgive them.	I will help you as you rely on My grace and forgiveness.	Be completely humble and gentle; be patient, bearing with one another in love . . . forgiving each other, just as in Christ God forgave you. (Eph. 4:2, 32)
No matter how much I do or how much I have, I'm never satisfied.	Don't spend so much money and time on things that can't satisfy your soul. Let Me give you what your heart needs.	Why spend money on what is not bread, and your labor on what does not satisfy? Listen, listen to me, and eat what is good, and you will delight in the richest of fare. Give ear and come to me; listen, that you may live. (Isa. 55:2–3)
I'm not really good at anything.	I have set you apart with unique gifts to equip you for what I've created you to do.	I knew you before I formed you in your mother's womb. Before you were born I set you apart and appointed you as my prophet to the nations. (Jer. 1:5 NLT)

When I Say	God Says	Powerful Promises
Will I ever conquer my fears?	I will help you as you help others.	Have I not commanded you? Be strong and courageous. Do not be afraid; do not be discouraged, for the LORD your God will be with you wherever you go. (Josh. 1:9)
I have no confidence left.	I will be your confidence.	For the LORD will be your confidence and will keep your foot from being caught. (Prov. 3:26 NASB)
My fears are paralyzing my faith.	Fear not, for I am with you. I have called you by name; you are Mine.	Do not fear, for I have redeemed you; I have summoned you by name; you are mine. When you pass through the waters, I will be with you; and when you pass through the rivers, they will not sweep over you. When you walk through the fire, you will not be burned; the flames will not set you ablaze. (Isa. 43:1–2)
I'll never be content.	Let My unfailing love satisfy the longings of your heart.	What a [woman] desires is unfailing love. (Prov. 19:22)
I feel like damaged goods.	You are royalty to Me.	You will be a crown of splendor in the LORD's hand, a royal diadem in the hand of your God. (Isa. 62:3)
What's wrong with me?	When you feel defeated or defective, stand on the promise that you are more than a conqueror because of My love for you!	In all these things [you] are more than [a conqueror] through him who loved [you]. (Rom. 8:37)
Everything and everyone is against me.	I am for you!	What, then, shall [you] say in response to these things? If God is for [you], who can be against [you]? (Rom. 8:31)
I don't know what God wants me to do.	Listen closely for My voice and follow the promptings of your heart that are consistent with My ways and My Word.	My sheep listen to my voice; I know them, and they follow me. (John 10:27)

When I Say	God Says	Powerful Promises
I don't want to hope because I don't want to be disappointed.	Let Me fill you with My hope as you trust in Me today.	May the God of hope fill you with all joy and peace as you trust in him, so that you may overflow with hope by the power of the Holy Spirit. (Rom. 15:13)
I just don't have it in me.	Let Me give My life to you and live My life through you.	I have been crucified with Christ and I no longer live, but Christ lives in me. The life I now live in the body, I live by faith in the Son of God who loved me and gave himself for me. (Gal. 2:20)
I feel so empty.	I created you with a longing in your heart that only I can fill.	Satisfy us in the morning with your unfailing love, that we may sing for joy and be glad all our days. (Ps. 90:14)
I'm so disappointed.	Let Me show you My ways in this disappointment and guide your emotions with My truth.	Show me your ways, Lord, teach me your paths. Guide me in your truth and teach me, for you are God my Savior, and my hope is in you all day long. (Ps. 25:4–5)
I'll never measure up.	Don't use the measuring stick of comparison; instead, measure UP by focusing upward on Christ—remembering who you are in Him.	He who began a good work in you will carry it on to completion until the day of Christ Jesus. (Phil. 1:6)
I'm not good enough.	You are covered in My goodness, and My goodness makes you good enough!	For your Maker is your husband— the Lord Almighty is his name— the Holy One of Israel is your Redeemer. (Isa. 54:5)
I feel so weak.	Don't let Satan wear you down. Protect your mind with truth, and pray in the power of My promises every day.	Finally, be strong in the Lord and in his mighty power. . . . Take the helmet of salvation and the sword of the Spirit, which is the word of God. And pray in the Spirit on all occasions with all kinds of prayers and requests. (Eph. 6:10, 17–18)
I can't stop thinking negative thoughts.	Let Me renew your mind and transform your thinking with My thoughts toward you.	Do not conform to the pattern of this world, but be transformed by the renewing of your mind. (Rom. 12:2)

When I Say	God Says	Powerful Promises
I've blown it and I feel so guilty!	Give Me the guilt, and I will replace it with mercy and grace to help in your time of need.	Let us then approach God's throne of grace with confidence, so that we may receive mercy and find grace to help us in our time of need. (Heb. 4:16)
No one cares about all that is concerning me.	Give your cares to Me, and let Me care for you.	Give all your worries and cares to God, for he cares about you. (1 Pet. 5:7 NLT)
I have lost all hope.	Put your hope in Me. My love never ends and My compassion never fails.	Yet I still dare to hope when I remember this: The faithful love of the LORD never ends! His mercies never cease. Great is his faithfulness. (Lam. 3:21–23 NLT)
I have nothing special to offer.	I have entrusted you with gifts and abilities to serve Me and others.	For if the willingness is there, the gift is acceptable according to what one has, not according to what one does not have. (2 Cor. 8:12)
I feel far from God, like I need to work my way back to Him.	I am here offering grace and truth to remind you there is no condemnation for those who are in Christ Jesus.	For it is by grace you have been saved, through faith—and this is not from yourselves, it is the gift of God—not by works, so that no one can boast. (Eph. 2:8–9)
I am battling fear and anxiety that won't go away.	Cry out to Me when you are anxious and afraid. I will rescue you from the grave of despair.	Then they cried to the LORD in their trouble, and he saved them from their distress. He sent out his word and healed them; he rescued them from the grave. (Ps. 107:19–20)
I'm not worth pursuing.	I am here, pursuing you with My love each and every day.	I have loved you with an everlasting love; I have drawn you with unfailing kindness. (Jer. 31:3)
I always let people down. I'm such a disappointment.	Keep your mind clear of condemnation, and be alert. Your opponent the devil is prowling around like a lion looking to devour you with doubt.	Keep your mind clear, and be alert. Your opponent the devil is prowling around like a roaring lion as he looks for someone to devour. (1 Pet. 5:8 GW)
My life is full of problems.	I will use all things, even the hard things, for your good and My glory.	And we know that in all things God works for the good of those who love him, who have been called according to his purpose. (Rom. 8:28)

When I Say	God Says	Powerful Promises
My needs are consuming.	Let My compassions that are new every morning consume and comfort you.	Because of the LORD's great love we are not consumed, for his compassions never fail. They are new every morning; great is your faithfulness. (Lam. 3:22–23)
I feel overwhelmed.	I will give you peace.	You will keep in perfect peace those whose minds are steadfast, because they trust in you. (Isa. 26:3)
I feel ugly and unwanted.	You are My beloved.	You are precious and honored in my sight, and . . . I love you. (Isa. 43:4)
I want to encourage others, but I don't know what to say.	Listen with your heart and I will give you the words they need to hear.	The Sovereign LORD has given [you] his words of wisdom, so that [you] know how to comfort the weary. Morning by morning he wakens [you] and opens [your] understanding to his will. (Isa. 50:4 NLT)
No one is there for me.	I am here for you, watching over you each day.	For the LORD your God is living among you. He is a mighty savior. He will take delight in you with gladness. With his love, he will calm all your fears. He will rejoice over you with joyful songs. (Zeph. 3:17 NLT)
I feel like such a failure.	Choose to fail forward by learning and growing from your failures.	Though the righteous fall seven times, they rise again. (Prov. 24:16)
No one sees me.	I see you. You are the focus of My love.	Long before he laid down earth's foundations, he had [me] in mind, had settled on [me] as the focus of his love, to be made whole and holy by his love. (Eph. 1:4 Message)
It's hard to believe God's promises are true for me.	Choose to live in the security of My promises, no matter what your feelings tell you.	Blessed is she who has believed that the Lord would fulfill his promises to her! (Luke 1:45)
I'm afraid to let go.	You can trust My heart. Watch and see how My splendor will be displayed in your surrender.	They will be called oaks of righteousness, a planting of the LORD for the display of his splendor. (Isa. 61:3)

When I Say	God Says	Powerful Promises
I'm not smart enough. My faith is too weak. I'll never change.	Don't throw away your confidence. Persevere in faith by replacing your doubts with the power of My promises.	So do not throw away your confidence; it will be richly rewarded. You need to persevere so that when you have done the will of God, you will receive what he has promised. (Heb. 10:35–36)
I'm beyond hurt.	But you are not beyond My reach. Let Me walk with you through these troubles and help you today.	Though [you] walk in the midst of trouble, [I] preserve [your] life; [I] stretch out [My] hand against the anger of [your] foes, with [My] right hand [I] save [you]. (Ps. 138:7)
I can't do this.	You can do all things through Christ who gives you strength. Keep praying and depending on Me for help.	I can do all this through him who gives me strength. (Phil. 4:13)
I can't stop worrying.	Take your eyes off your worries and focus on worshiping Me instead, remembering that I can accomplish all that concerns you.	Don't worry about anything; instead, pray about everything. (Phil. 4:6 NLT)
I'm a mess. How can God keep His promises to me?	My promises have no conditions. You have a lifetime warranty with Me.	For no matter how many promises God has made, they are "Yes" in Christ. . . . Now it is God who makes both us and you stand firm in Christ. He anointed us, set his seal of ownership on us, and put his Spirit in our hearts as a deposit, guaranteeing what is to come. (2 Cor. 1:20–22)

LEADING WOMEN TO LIVE CONFIDENTLY IN CHRIST

Renee Swope is the author of *A Confident Heart*, a 2012 Retailers Choice Award–winner and CBA bestseller that sold over 50,000 copies during its first year in print. She is also co-host of Proverbs 31 Ministries' international radio program, where she connects with millions of women from around the world each week through personal stories and biblical truths.

Renee's passion is to help women live confidently in Christ by showing them how to rely on and live in the security of God's promises. She is a popular blogger and host of online book studies on her website, where she's led over 25,000 women through *A Confident Heart* on her blog.

She is also a featured writer for Proverbs 31 Ministries' *Encouragement for Today* devotions that reach over half a million readers each day through the ministry's website as well as BibleGateway.com, Crosswalk.com, ChristianityToday.com, and Growthtrac.com.

Renee has been married for over twenty years and is a mom of three. She traveled with her family to Africa in 2010 to bring home their beautiful daughter whom they adopted from Ethiopia at the age of ten months. They live in North Carolina, where she also serves as an executive director with Proverbs 31 Ministries.

Much like her written words, Renee's messages come from a heart that has been transformed by the power of God's love and grace. Sprinkled with humor and saturated with truth, Renee's conferences are filled with biblical insights that are powerful and life applications that are practical. Invite Renee to speak at your next women's event—your audience will be challenged as women and encouraged as children of God!

For more information or to personally connect with Renee, visit her interactive website:
www.ReneeSwope.com

Proverbs 31
MINISTRIES

If you were inspired by *A Confident Heart Devotional* and yearn to deepen your personal relationship with Jesus Christ, we encourage you to connect with Proverbs 31 Ministries, where Renee serves as an executive director and radio show co-host. Proverbs 31 Ministries exists to be a trusted friend who will take you by the hand and walk by your side, leading you one step closer to the heart of God through:

- *Encouragement for Today*, online daily devotions
- Daily radio programs
- Books and resources
- Dynamic speakers with life-changing messages
- Online Bible studies

To learn more about Proverbs 31 Ministries,
visit www.Proverbs31.org.

Proverbs 31 Ministries
630 Team Road
Matthews, NC 28105
www.Proverbs31.org

Notes

Chapter 3 When Life Is Hard

1. Lysa TerKeurst, *Becoming More Than a Good Bible Study Girl* (Grand Rapids: Zondervan, 2009), 145. Lysa also offers a free downloadable resource on her website at www.LysaTerKeurst.com titled "When God Hurts My Feelings," which offers additional insights to help you process your "why" questions with God.

Chapter 8 Becoming the Woman God Created You to Be

1. Florence Littauer, *Personality Plus* (Grand Rapids: Revell, 1992).

Chapter 10 How Are You, Really?

1. Melanie Moore, "The 'I'm Fine' Masquerade," *Only a Breath*, posted November 1, 2011, http://www.onlyabreath.com/2011/11/thremoving-the-im-fine-mask/. For more encouragement, visit my friend Melanie online at www.onlyabreath.com.

Chapter 15 It's Over

1. "Light of the World (Here I Am to Worship)" by Tim Hughes, © 2000 by Thankyou Music. All rights reserved.

2. Part of today's devotion by my friend Samantha Evilsizer originally appeared in her Proverbs 31 Ministries *Encouragement for Today* devotion, "It's Over," March 18, 2013. All rights reserved.

Chapter 23 Letting God Rebuild Your Confidence

1. My friend Amy Carroll's story originally appeared in her Proverbs 31 Ministries *Encouragement for Today* devotion, "Rebuilt," August 24, 2011. All rights reserved.

Chapter 28 If God Is for Me . . .

1. "God Is In Control," © 1993 by Twila Paris. All rights reserved. From *He Is Exalted: Live Worship CD*.

Chapter 33 Dealing with Disappointments

1. My friend Tracie Miles' story originally appeared in her Proverbs 31 Ministries *Encouragement for Today* devotion, "Faith over Feelings," September 2, 2011. All rights reserved.

Chapter 34 Measuring Up

1. Dr. Neil T. Anderson, *Victory Over the Darkness* (Ventura, CA: Regal Books, 1990), 48.

Chapter 36 Before the Battle Begins

1. Julie Gillies' story is adapted with permission from her book *Prayers for a Woman's Soul* (Eugene, OR: Harvest House, 2013). All rights reserved.
2. Ibid.

Chapter 40 Dare to Hope

1. My friend Wendy Pope's story and part of today's devotion were originally featured in her Proverbs 31 Ministries *Encouragement for Today* devotion, "Dare to Hope," February 11, 2013. All rights reserved.

Chapter 42 When You Feel Far from God

1. Dr. Neil T. Anderson, "Daily In Christ," posted August 10, 2010, http://www.crosswalk.com/devotionals/dailyinchrist/544718/.

Chapter 43 Freedom from the Grave

1. My friend Stephanie Clayton's story originally appeared in her Proverbs 31 Ministries *Encouragement for Today* devotion, "Stressed-Less Living," March 15, 2013. All rights reserved.

Chapter 46 Shipwrecked

1. My friend Micca Campbell's story originally appeared in her Proverbs 31 Ministries *Encouragement for Today* devotion, "Arise from the Wreckage," August 23, 2011. All rights reserved.

Chapter 48 Peace-full

1. As quoted in Linda Dillow, *Calm My Anxious Heart* (Colorado Springs: NavPress, 2007), 123.

2. As quoted in Max Lucado, *Come Thirsty* (Nashville: W Publishing Group, 2004), 101.

Chapter 49 Remind Me Who I Am

1. My friend Glynnis Whitwer's story originally appeared in her Proverbs 31 Ministries *Encouragement for Today* devotion, "Remind Me Who I Am," February 6, 2013. All rights reserved.

Chapter 54 Mistaken Identity

1. My friend Karen Ehman's story originally appeared in her Proverbs 31 Ministries *Encouragement for Today* devotion, "Mistaken Identity," July 26, 2012. All rights reserved.

Chapter 57 I'm beyond Hurt

1. My friend Melissa Taylor's story originally appeared in her Proverbs 31 Ministries *Encouragement for Today* devotion, "I'm Beyond Hurt," February 1, 2012. All rights reserved.

JOIN RENEE

for personal encouragement to help you live with a confident heart!

Visit ReneeSwope.com

to download free resources and watch videos to enhance your personal study, share with your small group, or contribute to your book club. You can also see Renee's speaking schedule or join the next *A Confident Heart* Online Study.

f A Confident Heart by Renee Swope
f Renee Swope • ✆ ReneeSwope

Step out of the shadows of self-doubt to live with a confident heart

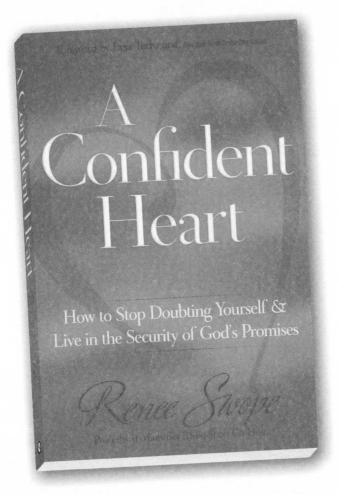

Ever feel like you're not good enough, smart enough, or valuable enough? Renee Swope understands. Even with a great family, a successful career, and a thriving ministry, she still struggled with self-doubt. Sharing her own personal story, Renee shows you how to rely on the power of God's promises to find the security you need and the confidence you long for!

Let Renee Lead Your Small Group
through *A Confident Heart* Study

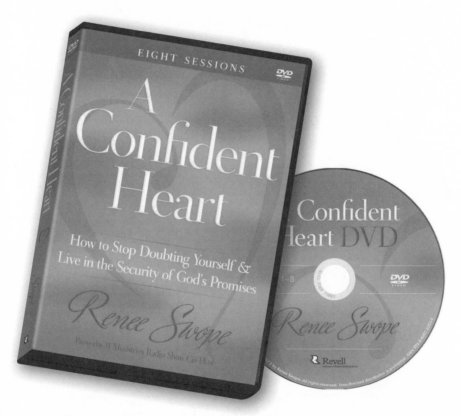

With perfect jumping-off points for focused and
life-changing discussions, the video segments on this
DVD will help you or your small group get the most out
of Renee's bestselling book.

**Free printable viewer's guide and
reflection questions are included.**